FAT-FREE COOKING

Delicious wholefood recipes to help you reduce the fat content of your diet.

FAT-FREE COOKING

100 Delicious Ways to Cut Right Down on Fat

by

SARAH BOUNDS

Illustrated by Ian Jones
Photography by John Welburn Associates
Food for photography and styling by the author

THORSONS PUBLISHERS LIMITED
Wellingborough, Northamptonshire
NEWMAN TURNER PUBLICATIONS LIMITED
West Byfleet, Surrey

First published 1985

© SARAH BOUNDS 1985

British Library Cataloguing in Publication Data

Bounds, Sarah
 Fat-free cookery: 100 delicious ways to cut
 down on fat.
 1. Low-fat diet — recipes
 I. Title
 641.5'638   RM237.7

ISBN 0-7225-1173-6

Printed and bound in Great Britain

ACKNOWLEDGEMENTS

My thanks go to Jacky Gibson and all at John Welburn Associates for their friendly co-operation with the photography. Thanks to Harrods, Lawleys and to Boots Cookshops for their kind loan of crockery, cutlery and glassware. Finally thanks to the National Advisory Committee on Nutrition Education (NACNE) for their report which has helped to inspire many to better health.

CONTENTS

1.

WHAT IS FAT?

Fat fuels the body. The energy expenditure involved in day to day living requires fuel from the food we eat. This it obtains, via complex pathways, from carbohydrate and from fat. We tend to think of a knob of butter, a slab of lard or a tub of margarine when we think of fat, but fat is found in many varied foods and although almost a quarter of the fat in the typical British diet comes from butter and margarine, the second biggest proportion comes from meats, with milk following close behind.

Reducing the amount of fat in the diet is not just a simple matter of being mean with the margarine on your bread. It also involves cutting down on other foods like meat, eggs, cheese, milk, cakes, pastries and biscuits — foods where the fat is hidden. We eat more hidden fat than we do visible fat so achieving a diet which is low in fat involves reviewing all the foods eaten, rather than just the fat we put on our food on the plate.

Whether hidden in cakes or meat or coming from a bottle of oil or a margarine tub, all fat is chemically similar. Fats belong to a complex group of substances called lipids. Lipids are found in many places in nature, not least in our own bodies. The fats we eat in food however are known as triglycerides, made up of glycerol and fatty acids. While glycerol always remains constant, fatty acids can vary and the specific fatty acid found in a particular fat will influence how it tastes, smells and appears to us. Most triglycerides mix different fatty acids together — each molecule consists of one part glycerol and three parts fatty acids, hence the name *tri*glyceride.

Explaining Fatty Acids
There are over forty different fatty acids found in nature. Although they are

chemically similar there are differences in their structure and it is these differences which underline the different forms of fats that we eat. These fatty acids fall into three distinct chemical groups, depending on their formula:

1. Saturated
2. Unsaturated or mono-unsaturated
3. Polyunsaturated

This method of classifying fatty acids reflects the degree of saturation of a fatty acid. Saturation is a term used to describe the chemical structure of a fatty acid. If there is one double bond in the formula, the fatty acid is said to be unsaturated or mono-unsaturated. More than one double bond in the formula means that it is polyunsaturated, and where no double bonds are present, the fatty acid is said to be saturated.

A fat consisting mainly of saturated fatty acids will tend to be solid at room temperature. A fat containing a large proportion of unsaturated or polyunsaturated fatty acids, will be likely to be liquid at room temperature. Fats liquid at room temprature are said to be oils but, as we shall see, oils are not always as unsaturated as they appear. Conversely, not all firm fats are as saturated as others.

It is worth understanding the chemical shorthand used to describe fatty acids as this reveals the degree of saturation. If the nutrition labelling of food improves, as the recently published COMA (Committee on Medical Aspects of Food Policy) report on diet and cardiovascular disease suggests, then formulae like these might appear on the packaging of food. Here are a few examples of some of the more common fatty acids:

Saturated Fatty Acids
   Butyric acid   C4:0
   Palmitic acid   C16:0
   Stearic acid   C18:0
Unsaturated fatty acids
   Oleic acid   C18:1
   Erucic acid   C22:1
Polyunsaturated fatty acids
   Linoleic acid   C18:2
   Linolenic acid   C18:3
   Arachidonic acid C20:4

The C represents carbon atoms, the first number indicating the number of carbon atoms present in the formula of the fatty acid. The last digit shows the number of double bonds. Hence linoleic acid has 18 carbon atoms and 2 double bonds, whereas linolenic acid has 18 carbon atoms and 3 double bonds.

It is particularly important to understand these two fatty acids because they are required by the body but cannot be synthesized by it. These are the two essential fatty acids. Arachidonic acid is also vital for health, but it is not regarded as an essential fatty acid because the body can make it from linoleic acid. As long as there is linoleic acid present in adequate amounts, the body will be able to convert it to arachidonic acid.

As long ago as 1929 experiments showed that linoleic and linolenic acid were essential for the growth and well-being of rats. In man we now know that these fatty acids are required for the production of a group of hormones called the prostaglandins which play diverse roles in the body. Because these two essential fatty acids must be present in the diet it is important never to eliminate completely all fat from the diet. Children have a particular need for essential fatty acids because of their growth rate, so take special care not to cut down the amount of polyunsaturated fatty acids in their diets.

Saturated Versus Polyunsaturated: the Heart of the Matter

The prostaglandins to which polyunsaturated fatty acids are converted perform a range of functions in the body, one of which affects the blood. Certain prostaglandins keep the blood consistency thin. Platelets can congregate together and form a clot; a degree of aggregation is obviously essential for blood to clot normally so that when bleeding occurs the body does not lose large amounts of blood from just a tiny wound. However if blood becomes too sticky then clots will form more frequently and easily. Such a tendency is increased by the consumption of saturated fatty acids. Not only does the blood become more sticky and prone to clot, but saturated fatty acids tend to increase the amount of cholesterol and other fats in the blood and hence increase the formation of fatty deposits on the walls of arteries. Eventually this will restrict the efficiency of circulation and will narrow the arteries, making it more difficult for blood to circulate.

This degenerative process is called atherosclerosis and it leads to heart disease, circulation problems and angina. Heart disease is the number one killer in Britain. We have one of the highest rates of heart disease in the world and things are not getting any better. Forty per cent of men and 38 per cent of women in Britain die from heart disease and strokes.

Atherosclerosis silts up the arteries with fatty deposits, putting extra burden on the heart to shift the stickier blood around the body. Under the circumstances a heart attack which is caused by a blockage in one of the heart arteries, or a stroke caused by a blockage in an artery in the brain, is far more likely to occur. Add to this high blood-pressure, where more force is required to move blood around the body; obesity where a high body weight puts an extra strain on the heart and smoking which reduces the efficiency of circulation, and there is truly a recipe for disaster.

However if you counteract these with regular exercise which improves the heart's efficiency by keeping your weight down, avoiding smoking and by cutting down on salt to help control blood-pressure, then clearly the picture becomes rosier. Health experts now recommend altering the fat content of the diet too, to help reduce the risk of heart disease.

It is worth mentioning here the term cholesterol. This is rather a red herring in the fat debate. It is true that a high level of saturated fats tends to increase the level of cholesterol in blood and hence the risk of atherosclerosis and, in turn, heart disease. However it is not exactly clear whether cholesterol in food will alter the level of cholesterol in the blood. Advice is generally given to restrict the level of saturated fats in the diet and hence the overall level of fat. Cholesterol in food is not now singled out for special attention, but much of the cholesterol in food occurs hand in hand with saturated fats, so restricting one often means the other is also limited.

Fats for Health

Much propaganda is published as advertisements and posters. There are many leaflets and booklets which purport to be unbiased, yet a glimpse at the publisher's name reveals that it is the margarine or butter boffins up to their old tricks again. The problem facing the consumer is who to trust in the fats war. To some extent the publication of two major reports has helped. First came the report from the National Advisory Committee on Nutrition Education (NACNE). Suppressed originally by government departments aware that its recommendations would have far-reaching effects on Britain's profitable food industry and farming community, the NACNE report was eventually published by the Health Education Council in 1983. Its dietary goals inspired many media articles and books which helped to put the facts about the food — and fats — that we eat into perspective. Then came the COMA report (Committee on Medical Aspects of Food Policy) on diet and cardiovascular disease, published by the DHSS in 1984.

Both reports favour a reduction in the amount of fat eaten. In both this is expressed as a percentage of the energy content of the diet. At present fat accounts for around 42 per cent of the energy in the British diet. NACNE calls for this figure to be reduced to 30 per cent, while COMA calls for a figure of 35 per cent to be achieved. Both single out saturated fatty acids; NACNE calls for the percentage of energy supplied by saturated fatty acids to be reduced from the current figure of 20 per cent to 10 per cent, and COMA recommends a reduction to 15 per cent.

Although the major reason for cutting down on fat, (particularly saturated fat) is related to the threat of heart disease, there are other excellent reasons for doing so.

Fat as a fuel for the body's energy activities compares favourably with carbohydrate and protein. Fat is twice as concentrated a source of calories, but in this country shortage of food is rarely a problem. Much more common and of increasing concern to health experts is the fact that 30 per cent of adults are well overweight. Eating large amounts of fatty food simply piles on the calories, and if the body has sufficient energy to meet its needs then it will simply store surplus in the body as fat. So cutting down on the amount of fat in the diet will help to control weight. Foods which are high in fibre and low in fat help to fill us up without adding too many unwanted calories. Following recipes in this book for a length of time will help to adjust your body weight. A low-fat diet isn't just a diet to help you avoid the threat of heart disease, it's a sensible way of eating for health.

Fats on the Table
The COMA report calls for more detailed labelling of food to give consumers information on the type and amount of fats found in the food. Hopefully by the time this book is published much will have been done to speed this along so that packaging will reveal the amount and nature of the fats found within its contents. This will help the consumer to cut down on fat and to avoid undesirable fatty acids. As already noted, whether a fat is predominantly saturated or unsaturated will determine its physical characteristics. The idea that solid fats tend to be more saturated than oils is about to be shattered! A glimpse at Table 1 (page 16) will reveal just how many margarines contain low levels of the beneficial polyunsaturated fatty acids and high levels of saturated fatty acids — some even higher than butter.

Not surprisingly butter supporters are frustrated by the commonly held belief that any margarine is a healthier alternative to butter. Margarines which are labelled high in polyunsaturated fatty acids are certainly better than butter but unless a manufacturer actually declares a high level of polyunsaturated fatty acids you can be reasonably assured that the product does not contain a noteworthy level of them.

Just because margarines are made from either vegetable or marine oils it does not mean that the end product contains any of the polyunsaturated fatty acids that might have been there initially. The margarine manufacturer needs to choose ingredients that will give his product the required consistency — either a soft spreadable tub margarine or a firmer margarine in a block. He may blend a high level of oils such as palm oil, which is already firm at room temperature, with liquid oils or he may simply choose any oils available at the right price and then process them to achieve the right texture. It is possible to make an unsaturated or polyunsaturated fatty acid hard, although it is usually liquid at room temperature. This is achieved by saturating the double bonds and so altering the melting point. Hydrogen is added to the double bond, saturating it, in a process called hydrogenation. The level of fatty acids declared by manufacturers in Table 1 and the level which may appear on any packaging will, however, represent the level present in the finished margarine. Another word which may appear on packaging is 'cis'. This refers to the form in which the fatty acid is found. There are two possible forms, 'cis' and 'trans'. Cis is the biologically desirable form, as the body will be able to use polyunsaturated fatty acids which are present as cis fats, but will be unable to use trans fats. Some polyunsaturated fatty acids are converted to trans fats during processing. This is yet another issue to confuse the consumer; again COMA labelling proposals should, when enforced, help to clarify whether the polyunsaturated fatty acids present are trans and therefore useless.

In a low-fat diet it is obvious that the amount of spreading fats used, like margarine and butter, should be reduced. When you do use a fat on bread make sure it is a margarine high in polyunsaturated fatty acids, rather than a margarine or butter high in saturated fatty acids. Similarly, processes like frying and roasting which add extra fat to food should be avoided, but a small amount of cooking oil may be required in certain dishes. Avoid animal fats like dripping, lard or butter and choose an oil instead. Safflower, sunflower, corn, soya or peanut are preferable to those with lower levels of polyunsaturated fatty acids. Avoid bottles which state simple 'blended' oil as these may well combine more saturated oils and are unlikely to be high in polyunsaturated fatty acids. Olive oil does not contain a particularly high level of polyunsaturated fatty acids, but does not contain much saturates either; it has rather a neutral effect as it contains mostly unsaturated fatty acids. It is also valued for its distinctive flavour required in certain Mediterranean dishes.

Table 1: Fatty Acids in Food Fats

Not all margarines and oils are high in polyunsaturated fatty acids. As this table shows, some contain large amounts of saturated fats. Figures were supplied by manufacturers or taken from McCance and Widdowson's *The Composition of Foods*, and show the percentage contents of saturated, unsaturated and polyunsaturated fatty acids (PUFA).

	Saturated %	Unsaturated %	PUFA %
Butter	61.1	31.9	2.9
Margarines			
Echo	32.5	50.0	17.5
Stork SB	32.5	30.0	25.0
Summer County	16.25	47.5	36.25
Krona	43.75	48.75	7.5
Tomor	37.5	53.75	8.75
Blue Band	23.75	48.75	27.5
Flora	16.25	31.25	52.5
Kraft sunflower	16.5	30.1	53.4
Co-op Good Life	23.0	29.0	48.0

	Saturated%	Unsaturated %	PUFA %
Prewett's tub sunflower	21.0	26.0	50.0
tub safflower	18.0	20.0	60.0
Vitaquell	11.5	18.6	52.3
Oils			
Coconut	75.9	7.0	1.8
Corn	17.2	30.7	51.6
Olive	14.7	73.0	11.7
Palm	47.4	43.6	8.7
Peanut or groundnut	19.7	50.1	29.8
Safflower	10.7	13.2	75.5
Sunflower	13.7	33.3	52.3
Beef dripping	43.1	48.3	4.3
Lard	44.0	44.0	9.5

2.

PLANNING A LOW-FAT DIET

If you are resolved to cut down on fat you will probably be wondering just how much is enough. If the recommendations of the NACNE report are to be followed then this will entail cutting your fat intake by around one third. So if you eat on average 2,200 calories then to supply the desirable 30 per cent of energy from fat, just over 2½ oz (73g) will be required. A calorie intake of 2,500 daily will correspond to a fat intake of just under 3 oz (80g). These figures are calculated from the basic equation that 1 gram of fat will supply 9 calories in the body.

The 100 recipes in this book are all designed to be low in fat, particularly saturated fat. This is achieved by following two basic rules:

1. Choose foods low in fat, especially those low in saturated fat.
2. Avoid adding fats in cooking and serving.

Choosing Foods Low in Fat

Much of the fat in the food we eat is hidden fat, so cutting down on fat means watching carefully for foods which might contain invisible fat. Meat, for example, is commonly eaten in the mistaken belief that if visible fat around the outside of a joint or steak is trimmed away the rest will be free of fat. This is not so, as all lean contains a certain amount of fat. The red meats — lamb, pork and beef are high in saturated fats and so are the products made from them. As shown in Table 2 (page 23) meat products account for almost one-tenth of the fat in the typical diet, while meats themselves account for around 18 per cent. Cutting down on meat and on the amount of meat products like sausages, meat pies and cold meats, will make a big difference to your fat intake.

If red meats are to be restricted or cut out of the diet then something is needed to replace them. Many find that poultry fills this gap well. Chicken and turkey are not only low in fat, but they contain some polyunsaturated fatty acids too. Game is another low-fat food, but duck, for example, can be fatty if the skin is eaten (this goes for poultry too so always remove the skin before eating).

Fish is becoming increasingly popular once again and while many people are beginning to reject meat and poultry on ethical grounds, fish living free in the oceans is a more acceptable and healthier alternative. Fish is classified into two groups, oily and white. If you think that perhaps oily fish should be excluded from a low-fat diet, then think again! Oily fish like mackerel and herrings contain particular types of polyunsaturated fatty acids (known as EPA and DHA) which help to keep the blood thin and less prone to unwanted clotting. Regular amounts of these fish should be eaten as well as the less fatty white fish like cod, plaice and haddock. White fish however is traditionally drowned in fat when cooked, so care needs to be taken in choosing methods of cooking which will not add large amounts of fat.

Dairy products are another undesirable fatty food. Most of the fat found in milk, eggs and cheese, is highly saturated and should be restricted. This does not mean suddenly banning all dairy foods from the fridge; rather it entails choosing dairy foods carefully.

Milk: full fat milk contains nearly 4 per cent fat, and Channel Island milk even more. The fat in milk can be easily removed in the dairy by skimming. The resultant milk will contain only 0.1 per cent fat and half the calories of the original product. Skimmed milk is becoming increasingly easy to buy. Many milkmen will now deliver fresh skimmed milk to the doorstep, while supermarkets sell either fresh skimmed milk or long-life carton products. Dried skimmed milk powders are sometimes available but make sure they do not contain added vegetable fats. Semi-skimmed milk is also available; this will have had some of the fat removed, and this too is available both fresh and in long-life cartons.

Cheese: hard cheese like Cheddar is made up of one third fat. Stilton typically contains 40 per cent fat while Continental cheeses such as Camembert and Edam contain only 23 and 20 per cent respectively. Not surprisingly it is hard to justify eating much cheese in a diet which is desirably low in fat. Few of the recipes in this book contain cheese; if they do so then the cheese is used in a small quantity as a topping and is one of the new 'breeds' of cheese now available. *Tendale* cheese is made to resemble Cheshire or Cheddar cheese while containing only 14 and 15 per cent respectively, compared to the standard 30 and 33 per cent fat usually found in these two traditional British cheeses. *St Ivel's Shape* Cheddar-style cheese contains approximately 16 per cent fat. *St Ivel* also offer low-fat versions of soft cheeses, either a smooth white cheese or cottage cheese and these contain considerably less fat than their conventional counterparts. Look out for cheeses sold as Quark or *Fromage Blanc* as they too feature lower fat contents. Wherever the word 'skimmed' is used this implies less fat is present, but subtle variations exist as products may be called 'low-fat' or 'reduced fat'. The same confusion exists with yogurt too, as yogurt may be made from skimmed milk or, at the other extreme, from full fat milk. Look carefully at the label. Clearer labelling is definitely required so that the fat content of foods can be easily established on the shelf.

Eggs: eggs have gained rather a bad image in recent years because of the cholesterol they contain. It is true that eggs supply saturated fat and cholesterol but they should not be eliminated from the diet completely because they are valuable sources of iron and of B vitamins. Try to limit their consumption and to use them in cooking where a little can be shared between a few people, rather than serving up a dish of scrambled eggs to each person. Free-range eggs are preferable because they have been produced by more humane methods.

Just as eggs should not be completely avoided, because of other nutrients they contain, so milk and cheese are important sources of calcium and of vitamins A and D. However some people are allergic to milk and others find that its tendency to form mucus in the body affects their sinuses and so they choose to avoid dairy foods.

Fibre: Like meat, fish and poultry, dairy foods are devoid of fibre. Much interest is now being paid to dietary fibre, once called roughage. The NACNE report calls for an increase of the amount of fibre in the diet from the present average of 20g a day to 30g. Animal foods do not supply any fibre; it is up to the plant foods we eat to provide us with this vital ingredient.

Fibre is essential for a healthy digestive system, to keep the contents of the intestines flowing freely so guarding against constipation. It is now thought that a good fibre intake and the avoidance of constipation may well reduce the risks of other more threatening diseases such as diverticulitis, appendicitis, hernia and bowel cancer. Fibre intake has also been linked to diabetes and heart disease, the former to help put a brake on sugar metabolism, the latter through its effect on the metabolism of cholesterol and other fats in the body.

Fibre is found in grains, pulses, nuts, seeds, fruits and vegetables and these ingredients are also useful for their comparatively low level of fat. Fruits and vegetables are valuable for the level of vitamin C, minerals and other vitamins they contain and they also contribute to the fibre intake of the diet. More significant though are the grains, pulses, nuts and seeds because as well as supplying fibre in good quantities they also supply protein. In diets where meat intake is being reduced it is important to make the most of the plant protein foods. These fall into three distinct groups:

Grains: wheat, rice, rye, barley, oats, millet, buckwheat.
Pulses: peas, beans and lentils.
Nuts and seeds: walnuts, almonds, Brazils, cashews, etc. and sesame and sunflower seeds.

In Britain wheat is our most important plant protein and for maximum nutritive value it should be eaten in the wholegrain form or as wholemeal flour where the nutrients present in the original wheat grain are preserved virtually intact. Refining wheat to produce white flour removes much of the fibre, vitamins and minerals. The same applies to other cereals too so always choose products like brown rice, pot barley, wholewheat pasta and wholemeal flour for cooking. Grains contain only small amounts of fat and so are valuable in supplying the vital protein our bodies need for growth and repair processes, without the large amounts of fat that meat and dairy foods tend to supply.

Peas, beans and lentils are similarly a good choice for a low-fat diet. Their low level of fat combined with their high fibre and protein levels make them important ingredients. There are so many different types of pulses that they are a versatile food. Lentils, different beans, dried peas can be used in many savoury dishes to take the place of meat or if preferred to 'extend' the meat so that less is eaten per portion.

Nuts and seeds are another important source of plant protein and contain fibre, but they are higher in fat than grains or pulses. However the fat is less saturated than that found in animal foods, and their rich flavour make them a valuable ingredient in composite dishes such as nut burgers and loaves.

When using plant protein foods a simple combining rule should be followed to ensure that the most is made of the protein contained within the foods. Two of the three different groups should be eaten together to balance each other out — so mix grains with pulses or nuts at a meal or mix nuts with pulses. Alternatively balance the protein in, say, grains with a dairy food, fish, poultry or meat. In other words mix either a plant food with an animal food or mix two plant protein foods together at meal. It is usually instinctive to mix ingredients together anyway to provide interesting meals.

Sweet foods often contain a surprisingly high proportion of fat and so it is preferable to keep desserts simple and to avoid processed cakes, biscuits and pastries. Concentrate instead on making the most of both fresh and dried fruits. Avoid chocolate and sweets — not only for their fat but also for their high sugar content.

Avoid Adding Fat
Having chosen the right ingredients make sure you add only the minimum of fat during cooking and serving.
Avoid
    roasting
    frying
    sautéing
as these all add extra fat and choose instead methods like
    poaching

grilling
steaming
braising
baking

as these are all successful without added fat.

Take potatoes as an example. Raw potatoes contain 0.1 per cent fat; mashed with margarine and milk they contain 5 per cent fat; roasted potatoes contain 4.8 per cent and converted into chips they contain 10.9 per cent fat. If they are boiled or baked in their jackets then the figure remains at 0.1 per cent fat — that is until greedy eaters smother them with butter at the table!

The secret of low-fat cooking is to keep added fat to a minumum and to compensate for any flavour loss by making dishes more interesting with the addition of herbs, spices or well-flavoured stocks. This will also help you to cut down on the amount of salt added to food, and this may help to control blood-pressure.

Several of the recipes in this book require ingredients to be sautéed. If liked a little well-flavoured vegetable stock can be used in place of fat, or a small amount of a vegetable oil which is high in polyunsaturated fatty acids (Table 1, page 16) can be used. As noted earlier the body needs polyunsaturated fatty acids, particularly linoleic and linolenic acid as these are essential to health, so a small amount of oil is necessary. These fatty acids are also found in small amounts in plant protein foods such as nuts, seeds and grains.

Often fat is used to make pies, pastries and other baked goods. Try to restrict the amount of pastry in the diet — after all, shortcrust pastry is about one-third fat, and richer pastries contain even more. Reserve such dishes for occasional special treats; the same is true of cakes and biscuits. Chapter 7 contains some recipes for baking which are lower in fat than most conventional recipes.

Entertaining guests usually involves the use of fat-rich foods as these tend to be linked in our mind with luxury. However if you enjoy entertaining and tend to do so rather a lot, start to ring the changes and serve low-fat dishes to your guests; they will benefit as well as yourself! You'll find plenty of special recipes in Chapter 8 for various formal and informal occasions.

SOURCES

Table 2: Where Fat Comes From
(Figures based on the National Food Survey 1980)

Carcass meats	18.3
Meat products	9.1
Liquid milk	12.7
Dairy produce (other than milk and butter)	6.1
Butter and margarine	24.7
Cooking fats	11.9
Biscuits, cakes and pastries	5.9
All other foods	10.4

Table 3: Did You Know . . .
Fat is hidden in many foods, sweet and savoury. These figures show the percentage of fat in the following products:

Product	Fat Percentage
Liver sausage	27
Salami	45
Pork pie	27
Sausage roll (flaky pastry)	36
Frozen potato chips, fried	19
Potato crisps	36
Roasted, salted peanuts	49
Mayonnaise	79
Chocolate coated biscuits	28
Chocolate éclair	24
Doughnut	16
Mince pie	21
Double cream	48
Cream cheese	48
Milk chocolate	30
Bounty bar	26
Mars bar	18

Table 4: Foods to Choose and Foods to Avoid

Foods to Choose

White fish — cod, plaice, haddock, etc.

Oily fish — mackerel, herring, etc.

Shellfish — prawns, shrimps, etc.

Poultry — chicken, turkey

Game — rabbit, pheasant, duck

Skimmed milk and skimmed milk products such as yogurt, soft cheeses and those made with low-fat milks

Wholewheat products — flour, pasta, bread

Wholegrain foods — buckwheat, oats, brown rice, pot barley, etc.

Pulses — beans, peas and lentils

Nuts and seeds — in moderation

Fresh fruits

Fresh vegetables

Limited quantities of vegetable oils and vegetable margarines high in polyunsaturated fatty acids

Eggs — limited use only.

Foods to Avoid

Red meats — pork, beef, lamb

Meat products — pies, sausages, processed meats

Hard cheeses — Cheddar, Stilton, etc.

Full fat milk and full fat milk products

Cream — single, double, whipping and clotted

Ice-cream

Processed cakes and biscuits

Snack foods — crisps and other savouries

Fried foods

Butter, lard, dripping

Chocolate

THE RECIPES

All the recipes in this book bear an approximate fat and calorie value. These have been calculated from McCance and Widdowson's *The Composition of Foods*. All recipes have been designed with a low level of saturated fat in mind. Because our bodies need some fat, that which is polyunsaturated from vegetable sources, some recipes include small amounts of oils such as sunflower, corn, soya or safflower which supply these vital fatty acids. Olive oil is included in some recipes for its flavour and it too contributes some of the important polyunsaturated fatty acids. Where recipes require vegetables to be sautéed for flavour this can be carried out using a small amount of vegetable stock or alternatively a combination of stock and oil. For convenience I make a quantity of stock and freeze as cubes in ice cube trays of the freezer. Individual cubes can then be taken out when required. Alternatively, in recipes where vegetable stock is being used, e.g. soups, use 1 tablespoonful of the stock for sautéing. Where recipes use oil for sautéing, stock can be substituted for a lower calorie and fat value — but do remember that a small amount of vegetable oil is needed to supply vital fatty acids (see page 12 for full explanation).

3.

BREAKFASTS

Breakfast like a king . . . so the saying goes. Today we all seem to be too rushed to take the time to sit down and eat a reasonable breakfast. For most families breakfast is a time of hurried greetings, a quick cup of coffee and then a rush for the door. A couple of hours later hunger strikes and that means a dash for the nearest cake or tuck shop. To avoid those mid-morning hunger pangs learn to start the day sensibly, at home with a proper breakfast. For most people the notion of a 'proper' breakfast conjures up platefuls of over-greasy fried foods — not surprisingly, few people nowadays indulge in them. There are alternatives, however, which will provide the body with fuel to see it through the morning until lunch-time and which do not rely on large helpings of fat.

The importance of adequate fibre in the diet has already been mentioned and choosing wholemeal bread in place of white sliced bread is the best way to start overhauling your fibre intake. In a diet where fat needs to be restricted, however, take care not to be too heavy-handed with the butter. Choose instead a soft vegetable oil-based margarine which is labelled high in polyunsaturated fatty acids and use sparingly. Be more generous, however, with your chosen topping — honey, sugar-free fruit jam, marmalade, yeast extract or perhaps some peanut butter. Croissants are a lovely treat but are forbidden to the fat-conscious; all those lovely layers are there because of the vast quantities of fat used in the baking! If you're bored at the prospect of plain wholemeal toast every day why not ring the changes with some of the more unusual breads now available. There are good wholegrain breads on sale which are really nutritious, retaining the full value of the cereal grain in its unprocessed state. Try your hand at baking your own loaves too (page 90). It's hard to beat the smell of freshly baked bread, and with practice it is possible to turn out top quality loaves and rolls each time.

Breakfast cereals are another valuable source of energy and can boost the intake of fibre and of vitamins and minerals if they are based on unrefined wholegrains. Avoid highly processed cereals with large quantities of sugar added. Watch out for the salt content of many cereals which contain a surprisingly high quantity. Muesli is a good source of fibre but may contain large amounts of fat-rich nuts. Follow the recipe on page 29 for a tasty fat conscious muesli mixture.

Most of the traditional British breakfasts are based on eggs. As already noted, eggs should be eaten in moderation because of the high level of saturated fat they contain. Yet there is a place for up to three eggs a week in the diet and in dishes like Breakfast Kedgeree it is possible to reduce the amount of eggs and still end up with a tasty dish. Dishes where eggs are the major ingredient however are less easy to adapt and are best omitted altogether. Instead of hot egg dishes, try grilled tomatoes served with lightly poached mushrooms, and, if you must, a very lean rasher of grilled bacon.

For everyday breakfasts home-made yogurt is a cheap and nutritious dish which can be served in many ways with fresh or dried fruits. For liquid refreshment choose fruit juices, herb teas or varieties of teas such as Ceylon which are low in tannin. Decaffeinated coffee is also preferable to standard coffee and there are many respectable blends now available, both instant and ground, to make this a pleasant substitute. Remember to add skimmed milk to your hot drinks in place of full-fat milk — or drink them black.

Yogurt

There are many different types of natural yogurt now available. For least fat and calories choose products which are made from skimmed milk as these contain only traces of fat. If in doubt, make your own. This is not difficult; the golden rules are not to add the milk at such a high temperature that it destroys the bacteria and, secondly, to leave the yogurt long enough to incubate, so the bacteria can do their trick and turn plain milk into the refreshing tanginess of natural yogurt at a fraction of the price of shop brands.

There are many yogurt makers on the market, but cheapest of all is the wide-necked *Thermos* flask. However you might like to buy a model with individual cartons as these are convenient for transporting and children like to have their own pot of yogurt.

Natural Yogurt

(Makes 1 pint/600ml. Supplies 0.8g fat and 260 calories.)

Imperial (Metric)
1 pint (600ml) skimmed milk
1 tablespoon natural yogurt
1 tablespoon skimmed milk powder

1. Place the milk in a saucepan and heat to 110°F/50°C.

2. While the milk is warming, mix the yogurt and skimmed milk powder and place in the base of a wide-necked *Thermos* flask or yogurt maker.

3. Pour heated milk onto starter and stir in thoroughly to distribute the starter evenly. Cover and leave to incubate for 6-8 hours. Release lid, and chill until required.

Yogurt is a versatile food, particularly so in a low-fat diet. It's distinctive taste makes it an ideal addition to salads and sauces where it adds depth of flavour without greatly increasing the fat value of the dish. Like the skimmed milk from which it is made, natural yogurt is valuable for its protein content which helps to balance the protein found in plant sources — grains, pulses and nuts and seeds. It also supplies calcium as well as useful amounts of B vitamins.

Yogurt is an excellent breakfast food. There are countless ways of brightening up a bowl of natural yogurt. Add fresh fruit for valuable vitamin C as well as fibre or dried fruits, which are not such good sources of the former but are excellent foods for boosting fibre intake. Here are a few ideas for breakfast time yogurt treats. All use ¼ pint (150ml) of natural yogurt as a base.

Banana Swirl: mash a banana and stir into yogurt with some seedless white grapes.
Honeyed Prune: soak overnight 2 oz (50g) prunes and then chop and stir into yogurt with 1 teaspoon clear honey.
Peach Dream: chop one ripe peach and stir into yogurt. Top with 1 tablespoon muesli.
Spiced Delight: grate one eating apple into the yogurt and stir in a pinch of ground nutmeg and a little ground cinnamon.
Raisin Glory: chop one eating apple into yogurt and stir in 1 tablespoon raisins.
Orange Extravaganza: chop the flesh of an orange into yogurt and add 1 tablespoon wheatgerm.
Melon Moments: dice flesh of a portion of melon into the yogurt and add a few sliced strawberries. *Illustrated opposite page 48.*

Apricot Tang: soak overnight 2 oz (50g) dried apricots, chop and add to yogurt with a dessertspoon flaked almonds.

Grapefruit Boat: chop the flesh of half a grapefruit, mix with yogurt and 1 tablespoon sultanas and pile back into the grapefruit half.

Gingered Melon: dice the flesh of a melon slice and mix into the yogurt with a pinch of ground ginger.

Own Mix Muesli

(Serves 12. Supplies 6.3g fat and 230 calories per portion.)

While it's nice to have lots of nuts to chew on in your morning muesli, too many will raise the fat level dramatically. Mix your own muesli using hazelnuts which are less fatty than the more usual almonds and walnuts. Add plenty of dried fruit and choose jumbo-sized oat flakes. *Illustrated opposite page 48.*

Imperial (Metric)
1 lb (450g) jumbo-sized oat flakes
4 oz (100g) sultanas
2 oz (50g) raisins
2 oz (50g) dates
2 oz (50g) dried apricots
4 oz (100g) hazelnuts
Pinch of nutmeg
¼ teaspoon ground cinnamon

1. Place the oat flakes in a bowl and stir in the sultanas and raisins.

2. Chop the dates, apricots and hazelnuts and stir into the bowl.

3. Add the spices and mix all the ingredients together thoroughly.

4. Store in an air-tight container. Serve with skimmed milk, yogurt, orange or apple juice and, add some chopped fresh fruit if desired.

Dried Fruit Compote

(Serves 4. Supplies a trace of fat and 160 calories per portion.)

Remember to prepare this in the evening so that next morning the fruit will be plump and spicy. Choose your own selection of dried fruits.

Imperial (Metric)
¾ pint (450ml) cold water
1 lemon
1 orange
2-inch (5cm) piece of cinnamon
¾ lb (325g) mixture of prunes, dried apricots, dried pears, apple rings, etc.

1. Put the water in a pan. Slice the lemon and orange thinly and add to the pan with the cinnamon. Bring to the boil, simmer for 2 minutes.

2. Pour liquid over the fruit of your choice and leave to soak overnight. Remove the cinnamon before serving.

Breakfast Kedgeree

(Serves 4. Supplies 8.4g fat and 350 calories per portion.)

This recipe contains fewer eggs than most conventional kedgerees to keep the fat level down. Arbroath smokies are free of colourings.

Imperial (Metric)
1 lb (450g) smoked haddock *or* Arbroath smokies
Bay leaf
½ lb (225g) long grain brown rice
2 oz (50g) button mushrooms
2 free-range eggs
2 tablespoons skimmed milk
Freshly ground black pepper
2 tablespoons chopped parsley

1. Place the fish in a pan with enough cold water to just cover. Poach over a low heat for 10-12 minutes until the flesh is just firm.

2. Remove the fish from the pan. Place the cooking fluid in a jug and make up to 18 fl oz (540ml) with cold water.

3. Place the water in pan and add the bay leaf, brown rice and chopped mushrooms. Bring to the boil. Reduce heat and simmer for 25-30 minutes until the rice is just soft and most of the stock has been absorbed. While the rice is cooking hard boil the eggs.

4. Flake the fish, chop the hard boiled eggs and add to the rice with the skimmed milk. Heat gently until the milk is absorbed. Season with pepper and serve garnished with parsley.

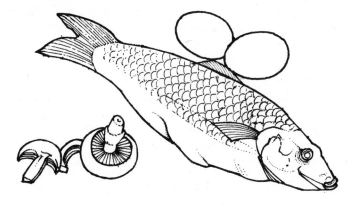

4.

HEALTHY LUNCH BREAKS

Whenever we have to find food in a hurry we tend to pile on the fat. Lunch-time for most people means a hurried sandwich grabbed from the local bakers or a hasty hamburger and bap from the nearest take-away. Instant food is often loaded with fat: fish and chips, Chinese take-aways, doner kebabs and the like all hide fat. If lunch is taken at home then there's always the temptation to fix a fry-up — it's quick and easy. If you're concerned about the amount of fat in your diet then you need to start afresh to make sure that the hungry hour in the middle of the day doesn't undo the good you're doing elsewhere.

Here are a few suggestions to help you on your way.

Sandwiches
Sandwiches are the obvious choice for a lunch-box and for lunch eaten at home too. Try to be mean with the margarine when spreading your bread. Choose a brand that is high in polyunsaturated fatty acids and spread thinly. Avoid the temptation of egg mayonnaise, cheese or ham — all fat fiends! Choose instead plenty of salad ingredients, low-fat soft cheese, peanut butter, prawns, canned salmon. Be adventurous and ring the changes by eating wholemeal rolls or pitta bread every once in a while.

Here are some tried and tested favourites:

- low-fat soft cheese mashed with banana
- low-fat soft cheese with chopped pineapple and beansprouts
- grated apple tossed with yogurt, chopped celery and raisins
- peanut butter with tomato and lettuce or alfalfa sprouts
- cooked chicken diced with avocado and yogurt
- shredded lettuce, chopped peppers, diced cucumber and tomato slices

Opposite: Healthy ingredients for a low-fat diet.

Don't forget open sandwiches. Choose either a crispbread or a Continental style bread such as rye or Pumpernickel. Arrange chosen topping attractively and serve fresh before the base becomes soft:

- tahini and cucumber with alfalfa sprouts
- low-fat soft cheese and orange segments
- button mushrooms and prawns
- baby beetroot with sliced green pepper and kiwi fruit
- soused herring with lettuce
- avocado and orange
- tomato slices, olives and pepper strips

French Bread Pizzas

(Serves 4. Supplies 4.2g fat and 430 calories per portion.)

A quick alternative to proper pizzas. The topping can be varied to include favourite foods.

Imperial (Metric)
8 slices of wholemeal French bread

Topping:

Imperial (Metric)
Italian tomato purée with herbs (enough to spread on bread)
1 green pepper
3 oz (75g) mushrooms
3 tablespoons sweetcorn kernels
4 olives, halved and pitted
Freshly ground black pepper

1. Place the French bread on a baking tray and spread thickly with the tomato purée.

2. De-seed and chop the pepper, wipe and slice the mushrooms and arrange on top of the bread with the sweetcorn and halved olives.

3. Place under a red hot grill for 3-5 minutes or if you already have the oven hot, place on the top shelf of the oven and bake for 10 minutes. Serve hot with green salad.

Opposite: Delicious low-fat ingredients for this family favourite. Baked Potatoes (page 35).

Pitta Bread

(Makes 6. Supplies 2.7g fat and 375 calories each.)

Imperial (Metric)
¾ lb (325g) wholemeal flour
1 teaspoon sea salt
1 oz (25g) fresh yeast
1 dessertspoon olive oil
1 teaspoon honey
8 fl oz (240ml) tepid water

1. Place flour and salt in a mixing bowl. Crumble the yeast into a jug and add the oil, honey and water. Stir until the yeast has dissolved and then pour onto the flour.

2. Mix the flour and yeast mixture together with the hands to form a dough.

3. Turn dough out onto a lightly floured surface and knead for 10 minutes until smooth. Place back in the bowl and cover. Leave to prove in a warm place until double in size.

4. Divide the dough into six pieces. It is essential that pitta bread is rolled thinly and baked at the top of a hot oven. Unless you own a fan oven where the distribution of heat is even throughout the oven, it is best to place one half of the dough in the fridge to rest and bake the pitta bread in two batches. Roll each piece of dough into a ball and flatten each ball slightly so it makes an oval shape, ¼-inch (0.5cm) thick.

5. Slide the ovals onto baking trays and dust the top with a little flour. Cover and leave to prove in a warm place for 20 minutes.

6. Light the oven 450°F/230°C (Gas Mark 8). Place empty trays in the oven to heat through and when the pitta bread has proved slide the bread onto these hot trays. Bake at the top of the oven for 10 minutes.

7. Remove from oven and leave to cool on a wire tray, before cutting in half and filling.

Baked Potatoes
Illustrated opposite page 33.

Potatoes cooked in their jackets have become very popular in recent years as a substantial snack but they are often served with fat-rich goodies such as sour cream and grated cheese. If you're a 'baked spud' fan there is no reason why you can't still enjoy potatoes, but go easy on the topping. Begin by substituting that lavish butter for a small amount of PUFA rich margarine and choose low-fat soft cheese topped with low-fat ingredients.

To cook the perfect potato heat the oven to 400°F/200°C (Gas Mark 6). Select good quality potatoes, allowing each person a potato weighing 6-8 oz (175-225g). Wash well to remove any surface dirt and prick all over with a fork. There is no need to rub either fat or oil into the skin — this is often recommended but I find potatoes bake perfectly well without either. Place them spaced apart on the top shelf of the oven and leave to cook for 1¼ hours until the skins are crispy and the flesh soft. Give the potatoes a gentle squeeze — wearing oven gloves to protect from the heat of the oven — to see if they are done.

Here are a few low-fat toppings:

- *Cottage cheese and pineapple:* For each person allow 2 oz (50g) cottage cheese and chop 2 rings of pineapple canned in natural juice and arrange on top of the baked potato. Sprinkle with parsley.
- *Low-fat soft cheese and herbs:* Allow 2 oz (50g) of low-fat soft cheese for each potato and mix with 1 tablespoon fresh chopped chives and 1 teaspoon chopped parsley. Alternatively, finely chop 2 spring onions and mix with parsley; or add 3 tablespoons sweetcorn kernels.
- *Italian Tomato:* Chop a quarter of an onion and sauté in a smear of vegetable oil. Stir in two chopped tomatoes (canned or fresh) and a sprinkling of dried oregano. Pile on top of the baked potato and top with a few strips of green pepper and some parsley.
- *Mushrooms:* Allow 3 oz (75g) button mushrooms. Chop finely and poach in a little vegetable stock with a squeeze of lemon juice. Season generously with pepper and pile on top of the potato. Top with a swirl of natural yogurt and garnish with parsley.

Soups
Soups are ideal for lunch-time as, served with wholemeal bread, they are filling and sustaining. Some soups take only a short time to make and can be prepared quickly; others needing more lengthy cooking can be made the night before and simply reheated when required. Because they can be carried in *Thermos* flasks, soups are useful too for lunches eaten away from the home, and especially warming on cold winter days. Don't dismiss soups during summer months though, as they can be equally as refreshing when made with the lighter vegetables of summer and can if liked be served chilled.

Courgette Cooler

(Serves 4. Supplies 1.2g fat and 46 calories per portion.)

Even if you don't serve this chilled, somehow the refreshing taste of courgettes helps to cool hot heads!

Imperial (Metric)
¾ lb (325g) courgettes
2 oz (50g) onion
3 oz (75g) potato
1 teaspoon sunflower oil
1¼ pints (750ml) chicken *or* vegetable stock
Bay leaf
Freshly ground black pepper

1. Wipe the courgettes and dice. Peel and chop the onion. Scrub and dice the potato.

2. Place the oil in the pan and add the onion. Stir around over a low heat for a minute before adding the chopped courgettes and potato, stock and bay leaf.

3. Bring the contents of the pan to the boil, reduce heat to a simmer and cook for 20 minutes. Remove the bay leaf.

4. Liquidize the soup, return to the pan and season with pepper. Reheat if serving warm, or place in fridge to chill. Serve with swirls of yogurt and a few thin slices of courgette if liked.

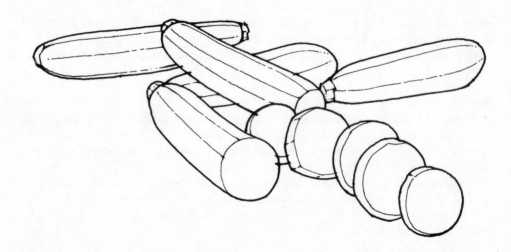

Parsnip Potage

(Serves 4. Supplies 1.5g fat and 120 calories.)

Parsnips replace the traditional leeks in this tasty version of the classic chilled vichyssoise.

Imperial (Metric)
1 large onion
½ lb (225g) parsnips
¾ lb (325g) potatoes
1 teaspoon sunflower oil
2 frozen cubes of vegetable stock
¼ teaspoon dried thyme
2 bay leaves
1¼ pints (750ml) vegetable stock
¼ pint (150ml) skimmed milk
Freshly ground black pepper
Parsley to garnish

1. Peel and chop the onion and parsnips. Scrub the potatoes and dice.

2. Place the oil and frozen cubes of stock in a pan and heat gently. Add the prepared vegetables and cook for one minute.

3. Add the thyme, bay leaves, stock and skimmed milk and bring to the boil. Reduce heat to simmer and cook for 40 minutes until all the vegetables are soft.

4. Remove the bay leaves. Liquidize soup and reheat, seasoning to taste. Serve garnished with parsley.

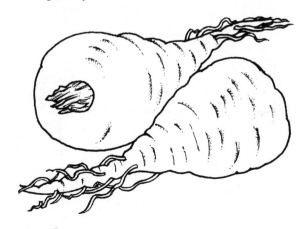

Lentil Soup

(Serves 4. Supplies 1.5g fat and 130 calories per portion.)

A protein-packed soup, the protein is made complete by the addition of a wholemeal roll. Indian spices add zest.

Imperial (Metric)
1 large onion
4 oz (100g) carrot
1 teaspoon sunflower oil
2 frozen cubes of vegetable stock
¼ teaspoon turmeric
¼ teaspoon ground cumin
Pinch of cayenne pepper
5 oz (150g) red lentils
1½ pints (900ml) vegetable stock
Bay leaf
Freshly ground black pepper

1. Chop the onion and scrub and dice the carrot. Cook gently in the oil and frozen stock cubes over a low heat for 1 minute and stir in the turmeric, cumin and cayenne pepper and cook for a further minute.

2. Add the lentils, vegetable stock and bay leaf, bring to the boil then reduce heat to simmer for 30 minutes until the lentils are quite soft.

3. Remove the bay leaf. Liquidize soup and reheat, seasoning to taste with freshly ground black pepper.

Country Vegetable Soup

(Serves 4. Supplies 0.4g fat and 95 calories per portion.)

The vegetables used in this soup can be varied to suit what's available.

Imperial (Metric)
1 large onion
1 clove garlic
2 sticks celery
4 oz (100g) carrot
4 oz (100g) potato
4 oz (100g) swede
1 teaspoon olive oil
2 frozen cubes of vegetable stock
1½ pints (900ml) vegetable stock
2 tablespoons tomato purée
2 bay leaves
Pinch of thyme
3 oz (75g) haricot beans, soaked overnight
3 oz (75g) white cabbage, finely shredded
Freshly ground black pepper
3 tablespoons chopped parsley

1. Peel and chop the onion finely. Crush the garlic. Finely chop the celery. Scrub and neatly dice the carrot and potato and peel and dice the swede.

2. Heat the oil and frozen stock in a large saucepan and over a low heat stir in the prepared vegetables.

3. Add the stock, tomato purée, bay leaves, thyme and drained beans. Bring to the boil, reduce heat and simmer for 1 hour, until the beans are almost tender.

4. Stir in the shredded cabbage and continue to cook for 10 minutes. Season to taste and stir in the parsley. Serve hot.

Creamy Mushroom Soup

(Serves 4. Supplies 1.8g fat and 70 calories per portion.)

It's hard to believe that this soup is made from skimmed milk — the result is beautifully smooth and creamy to taste.

Imperial (Metric)
2 oz (50g) onion
4 oz (100g) potato
1 teaspoon sunflower oil
10 oz (275g) button mushrooms, chopped
½ teaspoon dried thyme or teaspoon fresh, chopped
¾ pint (450ml) skimmed milk
½ pint (300ml) vegetable or chicken stock
Bay leaf
Freshly ground black pepper
Parsley or chives to garnish

1. Peel and finely chop the onion. Scrub and dice the potato. Cook gently in the oil for 1 minute.

2. Add the mushrooms, thyme, skimmed milk, stock and bay leaf. Bring to the boil. Reduce heat to a simmer and cook 25 minutes.

3. Remove bay leaf. Liquidize soup, reheat, seasoning to taste with freshly ground black pepper. Serve garnished with chopped parsley or chives.

Salads
Just as soups should not be confined to winter months, salads should form an important part of your diet throughout the year. There is an almost endless variation to the salad; gone are the days when most people conjured with lettuce, cucumber and tomato to produce one. Now all manner of vegetables, fruits, nuts, seeds, pulses and grains, as well as animal foods, are used in salads. Here are just a few recipes which are perfect for lunch. Slightly more substantial than side salads which are designed to accompany other dishes, these six salads all contain protein-based foods. The salads are accompanied by a selection of low-fat dressings; oils such as olive and sunflower have been used for their nutritional properties as well as flavouring, but unnecessarily fatty dressings such as mayonnaise have been omitted. Many salads can be packed up in air-tight boxes for picnics or to brighten up any lunch-time at the office.

Mediterranean Salad

(Serves 4. Supplies 6.4g fat and 200 calories per portion.)

Imperial (Metric)
¾ lb (325g) French beans
5 oz (150g) wholewheat pasta shells
1 tablespoon olive oil
Juice of ½ lemon
½ teaspoon dried oregano or 1 teaspoon fresh
Freshly ground black pepper
3 ripe tomatoes
1 green pepper
2 oz (50g) button mushrooms
6 black olives, halved and pitted

1. Trim the French beans and steam or boil in a little water for 5-8 minutes until just tender. Drain.

2. While they are cooking plunge the pasta into boiling water and cook for 10-12 minutes.

3. Have ready a screw-top jar containing the oil, lemon juice, oregano and a little freshly ground black pepper. Drain the pasta and then shake the dressing ingredients together and pour over beans and pasta.

4. Chop the tomatoes, de-seed and chop the pepper and slice the mushrooms. Add to the bowl.

5. Decorate with olives and serve when the pasta and beans have chilled.

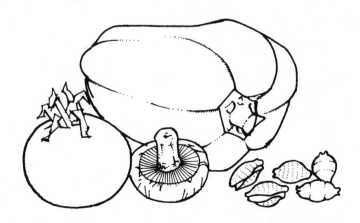

Hawaiian Rice Salad

(Serves 4. Supplies 0.5g fat and 100 calories per portion.)

Vegetarians can omit the prawns and still enjoy this tasty salad.

Imperial (Metric)
6 oz (175g) long grain brown rice
2 oz (50g) button mushrooms, chopped
1 red pepper
4 pineapple rings, canned in natural juice
4 oz (100g) peeled prawns
2 bananas
1 tablespoon chopped chives
Freshly ground black pepper

1. Place the rice in a pan with ¾ pint (450ml) cold water. Cook until almost soft and add the chopped mushrooms to the pan. Turn off heat and let the mushrooms and rice finish cooking in the steam. When rice is ready remove from pan and place in a salad bowl.

2. De-seed and chop the pepper and chop the pineapple. Add to the rice with the prawns and let the mixture cool.

3. When mixture is cold slice the bananas into the bowl and add the chives. Season with freshly ground black pepper, toss together and serve.

Caraway Coleslaw

(Serves 4. Under ½g fat and 45 calories per portion.)

If you don't like the taste of caraway substitute a little dried thyme in its place.

Imperial (Metric)
½ lb (225g) carrots
½ lb (225g) white cabbage
3 spring onions
2 eating apples
3 tablespoons yogurt
½ teaspoon caraway seeds *or* ¼ teaspoon dried thyme plus 1 tablespoon
    fresh chopped parsley
Freshly ground black pepper

1. Scrub the carrots and grate them into a bowl. Finely shred the cabbage or coarsely grate it if you prefer. Mix the two together.

2. Trim the spring onions and cut into fine rings. Add to the bowl.

3. Grate the apples — discarding the core — and add to the bowl. Pour over the yogurt and stir in the caraway seeds or thyme and parsley. Season with pepper and serve.

Beanshoot and Banana Salad

(Serves 4. Supplies 9g fat and 170 calories per portion.)

Imperial (Metric)
6 oz (175g) carrots
1 red pepper
2 handsful beanshoots
2 oz (50g) peanuts
2 oz (50g) sultanas
2 bananas
Juice of ½ lemon
1 tablespoon sunflower oil
Pinch of paprika
Freshly ground black pepper

1. Scrub the carrots and grate into a bowl. De-seed and chop the pepper and add to the carrots with the beanshoots, peanuts and sultanas.

2. Peel the bananas and slice finely into the salad bowl.

3. In a screw-top jar place the lemon juice with the oil, paprika and a little freshly ground black pepper. Shake vigorously and pour over the salad. Serve at once.

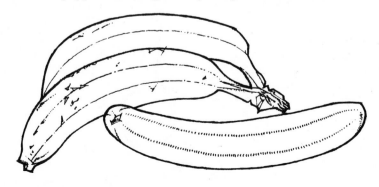

Creamy Cumin Salad

(Serves 4. Supplies 0.5g fat and 160 calories per portion.)

Imperial (Metric)
5 oz (150g) wholewheat macaroni
4-inch (10cm) piece of cucumber
1 green pepper
2 red eating apples
Lemon juice, to prevent apples browning
3 tablespoons low-fat yogurt
¾ teaspoon ground cumin seeds
Pinch of cayenne pepper
Freshly ground black pepper

1. Plunge the pasta into boiling water and cook for 10-12 minutes until almost soft. Drain and set aside.

2. Finely dice the cucumber, de-seed and chop the pepper and peel, core and dice the apples. Toss the apples in the lemon juice.

3. Mix the pasta with the prepared vegetables and apples in a bowl and pour over the yogurt, cumin, cayenne pepper and season with pepper. Chill before serving.

Chicken and Celery Toss

(Serves 4. Supplies 2.4g fat and 180 calories per portion.)

Imperial (Metric)
10 oz (275g) cooked chicken
4 sticks celery
2 oz (50g) raisins
1 green pepper
2 tablespoons low-fat yogurt
2 tablespoons low-fat soft cheese
Few drops of *Tabasco* sauce
Generous pinch of cayenne pepper
Freshly ground black pepper

1. Cut the chicken into bite-sized pieces. Chop the celery finely and mix together with the chicken and raisins.

2. De-seed and finely chop the pepper and add to the other ingredients.

3. In a separate bowl blend the cheese with the yogurt, *Tabasco*, cayenne pepper and season with freshly ground black pepper. Pour over salad and toss thoroughly. Serve on a bed of shredded lettuce with wholemeal bread.

5.

MAIN COURSES

The main meal of the day is also the most important meal. At this meal we consume more food and so obtain more nutrients. The success of a low-fat diet is very much determined by the type of food eaten each evening or lunch-time as the main meal of the day. Obviously we have to watch out for hidden fat at breakfast and lighter meals and snacks, but the day's main course is the most important one.

This chapter includes a wide range of dishes designed for everyday use. Chapter 8, Entertaining Ideas, includes dishes which have that 'something special' to impress guests but there's no reason why many of the more economical dishes found in this chapter cannot also be used for entertaining too.

One of the keys to a successful diet is variety and in this section there are many simple ideas which can be altered to create different dishes. Most recipes are vegetarian but for those not wanting to cut out animal foods altogether there are also recipes which contain poultry or fish and which are low in fat. Surprisingly, continental lentils are an excellent alternative to fatty mince, and are just as versatile as this standby favourite. Using these small round brown lentils in place of minced beef in Bolognese-type sauces produces a tasty sauce which can be used with pasta, rice, as a stuffing, or as it appears here in Shepherdess Pie (page 58).

Other members of the pulse family are also valuable in low-fat main meals. There are many varieties of beans in many shapes, sizes and colours. Used whole or cooked and mashed to a purée they can form the basis of many dishes for winter and summer meals. Different types of grain are also valuable as substitutes for rice to ring the changes.

Stocks
Home-made stocks win hands down for flavour but can be time consuming.

However once the ingredients have been prepared the stock needs little attention and can be left alone to cook slowly — or can be cooked more economically in a pressure cooker. Remember to strain the stock and leave it to cool so that any fat can be skimmed off and discarded. Freeze the stock as ice cubes for use in recipes in place of traditional fat or oil, or use as a tasty base for soups, sauces and casseroles. There are many excellent stock cubes now available but watch out for hidden salt; choose low-salt vegetable stock cubes available from health food stores in preference to those high in artificial additives and salt. Stock cubes can also be reconstituted and frozen for later use. Make sure other members of the family know which ice cubes in the freezer are frozen stock and which are water!

Chicken Stock

Imperial (Metric)
1 chicken carcass
2 pints (1.2 litres) water
1 onion
4 oz (100g) carrots
1 stick celery
2 bay leaves
6 black peppercorns
1 sprig of fresh thyme *or* ½ teaspoon dried

1. Place the chicken carcass in a large saucepan with the water.

2. Roughly chop the onion. Scrub and dice the carrots, chop the celery.

3. Add the prepared vegetables to the pan with the bay leaves, peppercorns and thyme.

4. Bring to the boil then reduce heat and simmer, covered, for 1½ hours over a very low heat. Alternatively pressure cook for 25 minutes at 15 lb (6 kilos) pressure.

5. When the stock is ready, strain and leave to cool. When cold skim off the fat. The stock is now ready to use.

Vegetable Stock

Imperial (Metric)
1 stick celery
1 onion
4 oz (100g) carrots
6 black peppercorns
1 sprig fresh thyme *or* ¾ teaspoon dried
3 parsley stalks
2 pints (1.2 litres) water

1. Chop the celery and peel and chop the onion. Scrub and dice the carrots.

2. Place all the vegetables in a large saucepan with the peppercorns, thyme, parsley stalks, and water and bring to the boil.

3. Reduce the heat and simmer slowly for 1-1¼ hours. Alternatively pressure cook at 15 lb (6 kilos) for 15 minutes.

4. Strain the stock and leave to cool.

Court Bouillon

This special stock is ideal for poaching fish.

Imperial (Metric)
1 carrot
1 onion
1 stick celery
1 bay leaf
2 sprigs thyme
3 parsley stalks
Juice of ½ lemon
¼ pint (150ml) dry white wine
¾ pint (450ml) water
6 black peppercorns

1. Scrub and dice the carrot. Peel and chop the onion and chop the celery.

2. Place the vegetables in a large saucepan with the remaining ingredients. Cover and bring to the boil. Reduce heat and simmer for 20 minutes.

Opposite: Start the day with a healthy breakfast. From the top: Wholemeal Rolls (page 90); Melon Moments (page 28); Own Mix Muesli (page 29).

3. Leave to cool before straining and using to poach fish.

Note: Salmon, turbot and halibut as well as more economical white fish (cod, plaice, haddock) are all excellent poached gently either in the oven or over a low heat on the hob until just firm. Never over-poach fish or cook at too high a temperature as the flesh will become hard and tough.

Fish Cooked with Potatoes and Yogurt

(Serves 4. Supplies 3g fat and 300 calories per portion.)

Imperial (Metric)
1 teaspoon olive oil
2 frozen cubes of stock
1 onion, finely chopped
1 clove garlic, crushed
2 tablespoons tomato purée
¾ pint (425ml) water
¼ pint (150ml) dry cider *or* vegetable stock
2 bay leaves
Pinch of basil
Pinch of cayenne pepper
1 lb (450g) potatoes, scrubbed and sliced
1½ lb (675g) cod, haddock or coley cut into 1-inch (2.5cm) cubes
½ pint (300ml) low-fat yogurt
2 tablespoons fresh chopped parsley
Freshly ground black pepper

1. Place the oil and stock cubes in a pan and heat gently. Add the onion and garlic and cook for 1 minute.

2. Stir in the tomato purée, water, cider or stock, bay leaves, basil and cayenne pepper. Now add the potatoes.

3. Bring to the boil and simmer for 5 minutes.

4. Add the fish and continue cooking for 15 minutes.

5. Stir in the yogurt and parsley and season with freshly ground black pepper. Cook gently for 3 minutes before serving.

Opposite: A selection of fresh fruits makes a healthy and delicious dessert (page 104).

Crispy Topped Plaice

(Serves 4. Supplies 4.8g fat and 200 calories per portion.)

The addition of a little low-fat hard cheese gives a crispy and tasty topping.

Imperial (Metric)
4 oz (100g) wholemeal breadcrumbs
2 oz (50g) *Tendale* or *Shape* low-fat Cheddar-style cheese, grated
Freshly ground black pepper
4 plaice fillets
Juice of 1 lemon

1. In a bowl mix together the breadcrumbs with grated cheese and a little freshly ground black pepper to taste.
2. Arrange the fish in a heatproof dish with 1 teaspoon cold water in the base and pre-heat the grill to red hot.
3. Brush the fish with lemon juice and cover with the breadcrumb mixture.
4. Dribble a little more lemon juice over the top and place under the grill. Cook for 10-12 minutes, turning down the grill if the top becomes too brown. Serve hot.

Mackerel with Mushrooms

Although fish like herring and mackerel are higher in fat than white fish the type of polyunsaturated fatty acids they contain are thought to help protect against heart disease. Wrap the prepared fish in foil to let the fish cook in its own juices, eliminating the need for extra fat. Spring mackerel are much lower in fat than those caught late in the year. The fat content varies from 5 per cent to 20 per cent so it is difficult to give a fat and calorie content.

Imperial (Metric)
4 cleaned mackerel weighing about 6 oz (175g) each
Juice of 1 lemon
Freshly ground black pepper
4 oz (100g) button mushrooms
2 tablespoons fresh parsley, chopped

1. Wash each fish thoroughly and cut off the heads if the fishmonger has not already done so. Light the oven 400°F/200°C (Gas Mark 6).

2. Rub the insides of each mackerel with lemon juice and season with freshly ground black pepper.

3. Wipe the mushrooms and chop very finely. Mix with the parsley and place inside the cavity of each mackerel.

4. Wrap each in foil and place on a baking sheet. Bake at the top of the oven for 20 minutes. Unwrap, and serve hot, still in the foil.

Lemony Drumsticks

(Serves 4. Supplies 5g fat and 150 calories per portion.)

Chicken drumsticks are a useful addition to packed lunch-boxes and picnics. This recipe is fast and easy.

Imperial (Metric)
4 chicken drumsticks
Juice of 1 lemon
½ teaspoon dried thyme
Freshly ground black pepper

1. Wipe the drumsticks. In a small bowl mix together the lemon juice, thyme and freshly ground black pepper.

2. Arrange the drumsticks on a barbecue or grill pan and brush with the lemon juice mixture.

3. Cook the chicken for 5 minutes. Turn and baste with the lemon mixture.

4. Cook for a further 5 minutes, baste again and finish off for 2 more minutes. Serve either hot or cold.

Chestnut Roast

(Serves 5. Supplies 2.7g fat and 220 calories per portion.)

An ideal vegetarian alternative to Christmas dinner, chestnuts are lower in fat than many nuts. Dried chestnuts, available from some health food stores, need to be soaked overnight before cooking, but they eliminate the lengthy shelling process involved when using fresh chestnuts.

Imperial (Metric)
10 oz (250g) dried chestnuts, soaked overnight
3 sticks celery
2 cloves garlic
6 oz (175g) onion
6 oz (175g) carrots
Grated rind of 1 lemon
3 tablespoons chopped parsley
1½ teaspoons dried thyme
1 lb (450g) Brussels sprouts
Skimmed milk to mix
¼ pint (150ml) vegetable stock
Freshly ground black pepper

1. Drain the chestnuts. Place in a pan with cold water and cover. Simmer for approximately 50 minutes until soft. Alternatively pressure cook for 20 minutes at 15 lb (6 kilos) pressure.

2. While the chestnuts are cooking prepare the other ingredients. Finely chop the celery, crush the garlic and finely chop the onion. Scrub and finely grate the carrots. Mix together in a bowl with the lemon rind, parsley and thyme.

3. Prepare the Brussels sprouts and cook until tender. Drain and chop finely. Season and mix with a little skimmed milk to make a smooth purée.

4. When the chestnuts are cooked, drain and finely chop them and mix in with the celery, garlic, onion and carrots. Mix in well with the hands as this helps to purée the chestnuts.

5. Add the stock and season with freshly ground black pepper. Have ready a greased 2 lb loaf tin. Place half the chestnut mixture in the base, add the sprout purée and then top with the remaining chestnut mixture. Cover with foil and bake in a pre-heated oven at 375°F/190°C (Gas Mark 5) for 45 minutes. Serve hot or cold.

Mushroom Stuffed Marrow Rings

(Serves 4. Supplies 7g fat and 160 calories per portion.)

Imperial (Metric)
1 medium-sized marrow
2 oz (50g) onion
2 oz (50g) carrot
1 stick celery
4 oz (100g) button mushrooms
2 frozen cubes of vegetable stock
4 oz (100g) wholemeal breadcrumbs
2 oz (50g) ground hazelnuts
½ teaspoon dried sage *or* 1 teaspoon fresh
½ teaspoon dried thyme *or* 1 teaspoon fresh
Freshly ground black pepper
¼ pint (150ml) vegetable stock
2 tablespoons sesame seeds
3 tablespoons cold water

1. Cut the marrow into slices ¾-inch (2cm) thick. Scoop out the seeds. Steam or plunge into boiling water and cook for 5-8 minutes until just tender. Drain.

2. Finely chop the onion. Grate the carrot finely and chop the celery. Wipe and finely chop the mushrooms. Sauté vegetables together over a low heat in the stock cubes, for a few minutes.

3. Tip vegetables into a mixing bowl and stir in the breadcrumbs, ground hazelnuts, sage, thyme and freshly ground black pepper. Bind together with the stock.

4. Place the marrow rings in a shallow ovenproof dish. Divide the mixture between the marrow rings and press into the centres firmly. Scatter sesame seeds on top. Spoon 3 tablespoons cold water into the base of the dish and cover with aluminium foil.

5. Bake in the centre of a pre-heated oven at 400°F/200°C (Gas Mark 6) for 30 minutes. Serve at once.

Sauces for Spaghetti
One of the simplest supper dishes is spaghetti topped with a tasty sauce. Choose wholewheat spaghetti because made from wholemeal rather than white flour, it contains more fibre, vitamins and minerals. It has a slightly nutty flavour. The same cooking rules apply: plunge into boiling water and fork through to prevent it sticking. Cook until *al dente,* that is, until almost soft, but with a little bite remaining. Many sauces for pasta can be made the day before and quickly reheated or can be frozen and thawed out before use.

Rich Vegetable Sauce

(Serves 4. Supplies 2.6g fat and 80 calories per portion.)

A meatless answer to Bolognese sauce. The addition of sunflower oil helps to boost the flavour.

Imperial (Metric)
2 cloves garlic
½ lb (225g) onions
2 sticks celery
½ lb (225g) carrots
1 dessertspoon sunflower oil
1 frozen cube of vegetable stock
1 lb (450g) fresh tomatoes *or* 15 oz (425g) canned
¼ pint (150ml) vegetable stock
1 tablespoon tomato purée
2 teaspoons oregano
½ lb (225g) button mushrooms, wiped and sliced
1 green pepper, de-seeded and chopped
Freshly ground black pepper

1. Peel and crush the garlic. Finely chop the onion and celery. Scrub and finely dice the carrots.

2. Cook gently in the oil and frozen stock for 2 minutes.

3. Add the tomatoes (skinned if fresh), vegetable stock, tomato purée, oregano and mushrooms and cook for 20 minutes.

4. Add the pepper and continue to cook for a further 10 minutes. Season with freshly ground black pepper and serve over spaghetti.

Chicken Liver Sauce

(Serves 4. Supplies 7.4g fat and 200 calories per portion.)

Chicken livers make a rich-tasting sauce that is also economical.

Imperial (Metric)
2 cloves garlic
½ lb (225g) onion
2 sticks celery
1 lb (450g) chicken livers
1 tablespoon olive oil
6 oz (175g) button mushrooms
1 lb (450g) fresh tomatoes *or* 15 oz (425g) canned
¼ pint (150ml) chicken stock
¼ teaspoon dried thyme
¼ teaspoon dried marjoram
1 bay leaf
½ lb (225g) carrots
Freshly ground black pepper

1. Peel and crush the garlic. Finely chop the onion and celery. Trim the chicken livers and dice finely.

2. Sauté all together in the oil for a few minutes to turn the chicken livers brown.

3. Add the mushrooms, tomatoes, chicken stock, thyme, marjoram and bay leaf. Bring to the boil, cover, reduce heat and simmer for 25 minutes.

4. Scrub the carrots. Finely grate them and add to the pan. Continue cooking for a further 5 minutes. Season with freshly ground black pepper and serve.

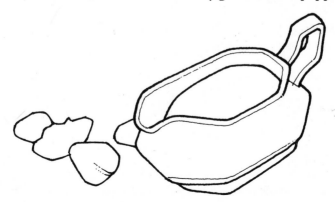

Mushroom and Pepper Sauce

Illustrated opposite page 80.

(Serves 4. Supplies 1.6g fat and 52 calories.)

Imperial (Metric)
½ lb (225g) onion
2 cloves garlic
1 teaspoon olive oil
Frozen cube of vegetable stock
¾ lb (325g) flat mushrooms
1 lb (450g) fresh tomatoes *or* 15 oz (425g) canned
1 large red pepper *or* 2 small
1 teaspoon dried basil *or* 2 teaspoons fresh
Freshly ground black pepper

1. Peel and finely chop the onion. Crush the garlic. Sauté both together in the oil and stock for 3 minutes.

2. Slice the mushrooms, skin the tomatoes if using fresh and de-seed and cut the pepper into fine strips.

3. Add the remaining ingredients to the sauce and bring to the boil. Reduce heat and simmer for 40 minutes. Season to taste before serving.

Spinach and Soft Cheese Lasagne

(Serves 4. Supplies 5.8g fat and 320 calories per portion.)

A classic vegetarian alternative to standard lasagne — just as popular with meat-eaters too.

Imperial (Metric)
½ lb (225g) wholewheat lasagne

Sauce:

Imperial (Metric)
1 clove garlic
4 oz (100g) onion
1 small red pepper
1 teaspoon olive oil
1 lb (450g) fresh tomatoes *or* 15 oz (425g) canned

¾ teaspoon dried basil *or* 1½ teaspoons fresh
Freshly ground black pepper

Filling:

Imperial (Metric)
½ lb (225g) low-fat soft cheese
¾ lb (325g) spinach
Pinch of nutmeg
Parsley, chopped to garnish

1. Plunge the lasagne into a pan of boiling water and bring to the boil; cook
    for 10 minutes until *al dente,* almost soft. Drain.

2. Crush the garlic, finely chop the onion and pepper and sauté gently in the
    oil. Add the tomatoes (skinned if fresh) and basil. Simmer for 20 minutes.
    Season with freshly ground black pepper.

3. While the sauce is cooking prepare the spinach. If using fresh, wash
    thoroughly, chop roughly and place in a pan. Cook gently for 4 minutes.
    Drain and chop finely. If using frozen, re-heat then chop finely.

4. Mix the spinach with the low-fat soft cheese and add the nutmeg.

5. Light the oven 375°F/190°C (Gas Mark 5). Place a layer of lasagne in the base
    of a lightly greased ovenproof baking dish. Add a layer of tomato sauce, then
    lasagne, then spinach and finally top with tomato sauce. Cover with foil and
    bake for 30 minutes in the centre of the oven. Sprinkle chopped parsley on
    top and serve.

Shepherdess Pie

(Serves 6. Supplies 1.8g fat and 270 calories per portion.)

The basic mixture of lentils with vegetables can be used in many dishes. Try it as a topping for wholemeal spaghetti, stir in cooked brown rice for a tasty risotto or use it to stuff peppers. Here it is topped with mashed potatoes to make a vegetarian, low-fat and economical version of a family favourite.

Imperial (Metric)
6 oz (175g) onion
1 clove garlic
6 oz (175g) carrots
2 sticks celery
6 oz (175g) mushrooms
1 green pepper
1 teaspoon olive oil
3 frozen cubes of stock
10 oz (275g) continental lentils
2 × 15 oz (425g) tins of tomatoes
¼ pint (150ml) vegetable stock
2 bay leaves
1 teaspoon dried marjoram
Freshly ground black pepper

Topping:

Imperial (Metric)
1½ lb (675g) potatoes
Bay leaf *or* sprig of mint
Skimmed milk (to mash potatoes)

1. Peel and finely chop the onion. Crush the garlic, scrub and finely dice the carrots and celery. Wipe and chop the mushrooms and de-seed and chop the pepper.

2. Place the oil and frozen stock cubes in a pan and heat gently. Stir in the chopped onion, celery, carrots and garlic and cook for 2 minutes.

3. Stir in the mushrooms, pepper, lentils, tomatoes, vegetable stock, bay leaves and marjoram. Cover, bring to the boil then turn down heat and let the mixture simmer for 40 minutes.

4. After the lentils have been cooking for 20 minutes, peel the potatoes and cut into pieces 1½ inches (4cm) across. Place in a pan with cold water and either the bay leaf or the mint. Bring to the boil, then reduce the heat and cook for 20-25 minutes until soft. Drain at once, remove herbs, mash with milk until smooth and season.

5. Heat the grill to red hot. Place the lentil mixture in the base of a heatproof dish and top with the potato. Place under the grill for 5-7 minutes until the top turns a crispy golden brown. Serve hot with a green vegetable.

Savoury Bean Ring

(Serves 4. Supplies 1.9g fat and 240 calories each.)

Baking this mixture in a savarin ring gives a convenient centre for filling with a salad. Alternatively bake in a loaf tin or shape into burgers and bake in the oven.

Imperial (Metric)
6 oz (175g) butter beans, soaked overnight
6 oz (175g) wholemeal breadcrumbs
2 sticks celery
4 oz (100g) onion
6 oz (175g) mushrooms
6 oz (175g) carrot
2 tablespoons tomato purée
3 tablespoons vegetable stock
Few drops of *Tabasco*
½ teaspoon dried marjoram
¼ teaspoon dried thyme
Freshly ground black pepper

1. Drain the beans. Place in a pan and cover with water. Cook for 1¾-2 hours until really soft. Alternatively pressure cook at 15 lb (6 kilos) pressure for 20 minutes.

2. When the beans are cooked, drain and mash to a purée. Stir in the wholemeal breadcrumbs.

3. Finely chop the celery, onion and mushrooms and stir into the bean mixture. Scrub and finely grate the carrot and add to the bowl.

4. Add the tomato purée, stock, *Tabasco*, marjoram, thyme and pepper and mix to a smooth consistency, adding a little extra stock if the mixture is a little dry.

5. Lightly oil a savarin mould and press mixture inside. Cover with foil, bake in a pre-heated oven at 375°F/190°C (Gas Mark 5) for 35 minutes. Turn out carefully and fill centre with a salad.

Butter Bean Goulash

(Serves 4. Supplies 0.8g fat and 230 calories each.)

Imperial (Metric)
4 oz (100g) onion
2 sticks celery
½ lb (225g) carrots
1 green pepper
1 red pepper
4 tablespoons sweetcorn kernels
½ lb (225g) butter beans, soaked overnight
1 pint (600ml) vegetable stock
15 oz (425g) tin tomatoes
Small tin tomato purée
2 bay leaves
1 tablespoon paprika
¼ teaspoon oregano
Freshly ground black pepper
Chopped parsley to garnish

1. Finely chop the onion and celery. Scrub the carrots and slice thinly. De-seed and slice the peppers.

2. Light the oven at 375°F/190°C (Gas Mark 5). Place the onion, celery, carrot, peppers, sweetcorn and drained butter beans in a casserole dish and pour over the vegetable stock and tinned tomatoes.

3. Stir in the tomato purée, bay leaves, paprika and oregano.

4. Cover and bake in the centre of the oven for 1½-2 hours until the beans are just tender. Season with pepper and serve with chopped parsley.

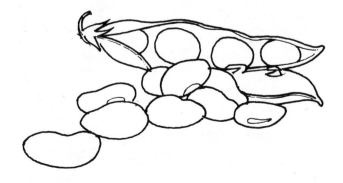

Boston Beans

(Serves 4. Supplies 2g fat and 200 calories each.)

A home-made alternative to canned beans.

Imperial (Metric)
½ lb (225g) haricot beans, soaked overnight
1 onion
1 teaspoon sunflower oil
1 tablespoon molasses
1 teaspoon mustard
15 oz (425g) can tomatoes
¼ pint (150ml) vegetable stock
1 tablespoon tomato purée
Freshly ground black pepper

1. Drain the beans. Place in pan and cover with cold water. Bring to the boil and cook for 20 minutes. Drain.

2. Finely chop the onion and sauté gently in the oil for 2 minutes. Stir in the molasses, mustard, tomatoes, vegetable stock, tomato purée and beans.

3. Bring to the boil then reduce and simmer gently for 40-45 minutes until the beans are tender. Season with freshly ground black pepper and serve.

Bean and Leek Braise

(Serves 4. Supplies 0.7g fat and 160 calories per portion.)

Black-eye beans are useful because they do not need soaking before cooking. They will cook in about 45-50 minutes.

Imperial (Metric)
½ lb (225g) leeks, trimmed weight
6 oz (175g) carrot
6 oz (175g) swede
1 eating apple
6 oz (175g) black-eye beans
1 pint (600ml) vegetable stock
½ teaspoon yeast extract
1 teaspoon fresh sage *or* ½ teaspoon dried
1 bay leaf
Freshly ground black pepper

1. Cut the leeks into ½-inch (1cm) thick slices. Scrub the carrots and slice thinly. Peel and dice the swede. Core and dice the apple.

2. Place all the vegetables in a casserole dish and add the beans, stock, yeast extract, sage and bay leaf.

3. Cover and place in a pre-heated oven at 375°F/190°C (Gas Mark 5). Bake for 50 minutes (check that the mixture does not become too dry and add extra stock if needed). Season to taste and serve.

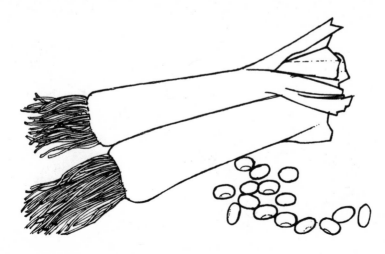

Winter Barley Hot Pot

(Serves 4. Supplies 0.4g fat and 160 calories per portion.)

Pot barley is more nutritious than pearl barley which has been refined. Health food stores sell pot barley — it's cheap, filling and ideal for warming winter stews like this one.

Imperial (Metric)
4 oz (100g) onion
½ lb (225g) carrots
½ lb (225g) swede
½ lb (225g) parsnip
1 stick celery
4 oz (100g) pot barley
1½ pints (900ml) vegetable stock
1 teaspoon yeast extract
1 tablespoon tomato purée
Pinch of dried thyme
Bay leaf
Pinch of marjoram
Freshly ground black pepper

1. Finely chop the onion. Scrub and slice the carrots. Peel and dice the swede. Scrub and dice the parsnip and chop the celery finely.

2. Place all these vegetables in a large casserole dish. Add the barley. Pour over the stock, stir in the yeast extract, tomato purée, thyme, bay leaf and marjoram. Cover and bake at the top of a pre-heated oven at 375°F/190°C (Gas Mark 5) for 1½ hours. Season to taste and serve.

Savoury Buckwheat

(Serves 4. Supplies 1.6g fat and 240 calories per portion.)

Use buckwheat in place of rice; cook with a good stock and some vegetables to add flavour. Cauliflower florets seem to complement this grain well.

Imperial (Metric)
2 sticks celery
4 oz (100g) onion
1 teaspoon sunflower oil
2 frozen cubes of stock
½ lb (225g) buckwheat
1 small cauliflower, broken into florets
2 bay leaves
18 fl oz (540ml) vegetable stock
2 teaspoons fresh sage *or* teaspoon dried, chopped
½ lb (225g) carrot, finely grated
Freshly ground black pepper

1. Finely chop the celery and onion. Cook gently in the oil and frozen stock for 3 minutes.

2. Stir in the buckwheat, cauliflower florets, bay leaves, vegetable stock and the dried sage if you are not using fresh.

3. Bring to the boil, cover and reduce heat. Simmer for 20 minutes until the liquid is absorbed and the grain is soft.

4. Stir in the grated carrots and chopped sage if using fresh, and season with pepper. Turn off the heat but leave the pan on the ring to stand for 5 minutes before serving.

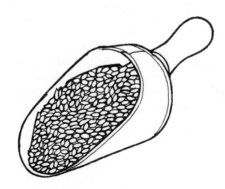

Sunflower Crunch Risotto

(Serves 4. Supplies 9.8g fat and 240 calories.)

Toast the sunflower seeds first to bring out their nutty flavour.

Imperial (Metric)
4 oz (100g) onion
Stick of celery
2 frozen cubes of stock
½ teaspoon dried thyme *or* 1 teaspoon fresh, chopped
½ lb (225g) long grain brown rice
1 pint (600ml) vegetable stock
Bay leaf
Small cauliflower, broken into small florets
4 oz (100g) courgettes, sliced *or* button mushrooms *or* sweetcorn kernels
4 oz (100g) carrots
3 oz (75g) sunflower seeds
Freshly ground black pepper

1. Finely chop the onion and celery. Melt the stock cubes in a large pan. Add the onion, celery and thyme and simmer for 1 minute. Stir in the rice and simmer for 1 minute.

2. Add the rest of the stock and the bay leaf. Bring to the boil, add the cauliflower florets and cover. Simmer for 15 minutes.

3. Lift the lid and without disturbing the mixture add the sliced courgettes, mushrooms or sweetcorn kernels and cook for a further 10 minutes (if the mixture looks a little dry add a little more stock).

4. Meanwhile finely grate the carrots. Toast the sunflower seeds either by heating a grill and placing the seeds in the base of the grill pan and toasting until just golden, or heat up a heavy-based frying pan (without fat) and heat the seeds until golden.

5. Check that the rice is cooked — it should be just tender without being stodgy. Add the grated carrots and sunflower seeds and season with freshly ground black pepper. If there is any surplus liquid in the base of the pan turn up the heat and let it boil away. Serve hot.

Walnut and Rice Bake

(Serves 5. Supplies 11g fat and 280 calories per portion.)

Imperial (Metric)
6 oz (175g) long grain brown rice
4 oz (100g) walnuts
6 oz (175g) carrots
4 oz (100g) onion
2 small red peppers *or* 1 large one
1 teaspoon dried thyme
4 tablespoons sweetcorn kernels *or* stick celery finely chopped
4 tablespoons tomato purée
1 free-range egg, beaten
4 tablespoons vegetable stock

1. Place the rice in a pan with cold water, bring to the boil, reduce heat and simmer for 25-30 minutes until just tender. Drain and set aside.

2. Place the walnuts in a blender and grind. Scrub the carrots and finely grate. Finely chop the onion and peppers.

3. Mix all these ingredients together in a bowl, blending thoroughly and evenly. Add the dried thyme, and the sweetcorn or celery and bind with the tomato purée, beaten egg and vegetable stock.

4. Lightly grease a 2 lb loaf tin and line the base with greaseproof paper. Add the mixture and press down firmly.

5. Cover with foil and bake in a pre-heated oven at 400°F/200°C (Gas Mark 6) for 35-40 minutes, removing the foil for the last five minutes. Serve either hot or cold with a crisp side salad.

Cauliflower with Cumin and Coriander
Illustrated opposite page 81.

(Serves 4. Supplies 1.2g fat and 55 calories per portion.)

Imperial (Metric)
2 onions
2 cloves garlic
½-inch (1cm) cube root ginger
4 tablespoons cold water
1 teaspoon sunflower oil
½ teaspoon cumin seeds
3 tomatoes, chopped
½ teaspoon ground cumin
1 teaspoon ground coriander
¼ teaspoon turmeric
1 large cauliflower, broken into florets
1 teaspoon garam masala

1. Peel and finely chop the onions. Crush the garlic and peel and grate the ginger.

2. Place 1 onion in the goblet of a liquidizer with the garlic, ginger and water. Blend to a purée.

3. Heat the oil and onion paste in a large saucepan and add the cumin seeds. Cook for 1 minute then add the remaining onion and cook 1 minute.

4. Stir in the tomatoes, ground cumin, ground coriander, turmeric and cook for 4 minutes over a low heat.

5. Add the cauliflower florets and stir in well. Add a further tablespoon of water and cover. Simmer gently for 20 minutes.

6. Turn off heat and add the garam masala. Leave to stand on the hot plate for 5 minutes before serving.

Prawn and Courgette Curry

(Serves 4. Supplies 4g fat and 250 calories per portion.)

Quick to prepare, this curry can be made with less chilli if you prefer a milder tasting dish. *Illustrated opposite page 81.*

Imperial (Metric)
1 lb (450g) courgettes
4 oz (100g) onion
4 cloves garlic
½-inch (1cm) cube root ginger
5 tablespoons water
1 dessertspoon sunflower *or* sesame oil
1 teaspoon cumin seeds
1 teaspoon ground coriander
1 teaspoon ground cumin
1 green chilli, de-seeded and chopped
Pinch of cayenne pepper
3 canned tomatoes and 2 tablespoons juice from can
1 lb (450g) shelled prawns
1 teaspoon lemon juice
Freshly ground black pepper

1. Wipe the courgettes and cut into fine sticks, 1 inch (2.5cm) long.

2. Chop the onion and garlic and peel and grate the ginger. Place all three together with the water in the goblet of a liquidizer and blend until smooth.

3. Heat the oil in a frying pan and add the cumin seeds. Let them sizzle and then pour in the garlic and ginger paste. Cook for 1 minute then add the ground coriander, ground cumin, chopped chilli and cayenne pepper and cook for 2 minutes.

4. Now add the tomatoes and juice and stir in the courgettes. Cook for 5 minutes.

5. Stir in the prawns and lemon juice and cook for a further 2 minutes. Season with freshly ground black pepper and serve at once, with plain boiled or spiced mushroom rice.

Black-Eye Beans with Mushrooms

(Serves 4. Supplies 1g fat and 145 calories each.)

Imperial (Metric)
½ lb (225g) black-eye beans
1 small onion, chopped
1 green chilli, chopped
½-inch (1cm) piece of root ginger, grated
6 black peppercorns
½-inch (1cm) piece of cinnamon
2 cloves garlic, crushed
2 frozen cubes of vegetable stock
1 teaspoon ground coriander
½ teaspoon ground cumin
½ teaspoon turmeric
1 teaspoon garam masala
1 teaspoon fresh lemon juice
6 oz (175g) button mushrooms
Freshly ground black pepper

1. Place the beans in a pan with the onion, chilli, ginger, peppercorns and cinnamon. Cover with water. Bring to the boil, cover and simmer for 20 minutes. Drain, reserving the stock.

2. Sauté the garlic in the stock for 2 minutes and stir in the spices. Cook 1 minute. Now add the lemon juice and mushrooms, drained beans and about ½-¾ pint stock reserved from beans (enough to make a sauce).

3. Simmer for a further 20 minutes until the beans are tender. Serve at once.

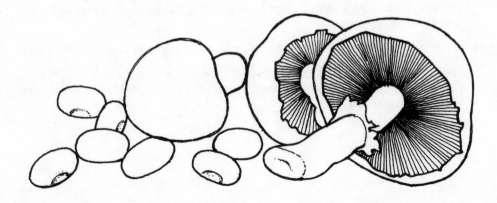

Spiced Rice

(Serves 4. Supplies under 1g fat and 225 calories per portion.)

This dish can be varied in many ways by adding different vegetables — chopped mushrooms, cauliflower florets, diced red and green pepper, a few cooked peas. This makes an excellent accompaniment to curried dishes. *Illustrated opposite page 81.*

Imperial (Metric)
4 oz (100g) onion
Stick of celery
Clove of garlic
6 oz (175g) carrots
3 frozen cubes of vegetable stock
½ teaspoon ground coriander
½ teaspoon ground cumin
¼ teaspoon turmeric
Pinch of cayenne pepper
½ lb (225g) long grain brown rice
18 fl oz (540ml) vegetable stock
Freshly ground black pepper
Fresh coriander to garnish

1. Finely chop the onion and celery. Crush the garlic and scrub and dice the carrots. Sauté all together in the melted stock cubes for 2 minutes.

2. Stir in the coriander, cumin, turmeric and cayenne pepper and cook for 1 minute. Now add the rice and stir so the grains become coated in the spice mixture.

3. Pour in the stock. Bring to the boil then cover, reduce heat and let it simmer for 30 minutes.

4. Remove lid, and test if rice is ready. If too much liquid remains, turn up heat to let it evaporate. Season with freshly ground black pepper and garnish with fresh coriander. Serve hot.

Potato-Topped Pie

(Serves 4. Supplies under 1g fat and 160 calories per portion.)

Conventional pastry is very high in fat. This recipe combines mashed potato with wholemeal flour to give a tasty topping.

Topping:

Imperial (Metric)
6 oz (175g) potatoes
Skimmed milk
Freshly ground black pepper
4 oz (100g) wholemeal flour

Filling:

Imperial (Metric)
4 oz (100g) carrot
6 oz (150g) swede
6 oz (150g) parsnip
1 small onion
1 stick celery
1 clove garlic
½ pint (300ml) vegetable stock
½ teaspoon dried sage *or* 1 teaspoon fresh
4 oz (100g) button mushrooms, chopped

1. Peel the potatoes. Cut into 2-inch (5cm) cubes, cover with cold water. Bring to the boil, then reduce heat. Cook for 20 minutes or until soft. Drain and mash with skimmed milk. Season with pepper and stir in the wholemeal flour. Allow to cool.

2. Meanwhile, prepare the filling. Scrub the carrot and cut into rings. Peel the swede and parsnip and dice finely. Peel and chop the onion, chop the celery and crush the garlic.

3. Heat 2 tablespoons of the stock in a pan and stir in the onion, celery and garlic. Cook for 2 minutes. Add the carrots, swede and parsnip and cook for a further minute. Now add the remaining stock and the sage and cook for 10 minutes. Stir in the mushrooms and season with pepper. Pour into a deep pie dish.

4. Roll out potato mixture on a lightly floured surface. Carefully lower over filling.
    Trim and brush with skimmed milk. Make a few air vents to let steam escape.
    Bake in a pre-heated oven at 400°F/200°C (Gas Mark 6) for 15 minutes, then
    lower heat to 350°F/180°C (Gas Mark 4) to finish cooking.

6.

VEGETABLE DISHES

Vegetables and fruits are vital ingredients in a healthy diet. Without them, we would receive no vitamin C. And without vitamin C our bodies would begin to deteriorate due to the deficiency disease scurvy. So daily servings of both fruits and vegetables are essential but so too is care in cooking. Vitamin C is one of the most fragile nutrients, easily destroyed by heat and by exposure to the air once the fruits or vegetables are cut. In order to make the most of the vitamin naturally present in vegetables and fruits take care to follow these basic golden rules:

- prepare as close to serving as possible.
- eat raw or cook quickly and lightly.
- cook either by steaming over fast boiling water or plunge into a small amount of water that is already boiling.
- eat as soon as produce is cooked. Keeping food hot destroys vitmain C.
- cut with a sharp knife rather than a blunt one.

Many ways of serving vegetables simply add extra fat. Be wary of smothering cooked vegetables with butter and avoid cooking methods like roasting and frying which depend on large amounts of fat for success. Instead simply boil produce, or steam, and make sure the main course of your meal has a tasty sauce or dressing to liven up the vegetables. Alternatively, look at some of the recipes in this chapter which add natural flavourings to vegetables to produce more interesting cooked side dishes. Serve vegetables as salads with low-fat salad dressings made with yogurt, lemon juice, vinegar and less oil than normal.

Carrot and Chervil Salad

(Serves 4. Supplies less than 1g fat and 30 calories per portion.)

Imperial (Metric)
¾ lb (325g) carrots
1 teaspoon chopped chervil or ½ teaspoon dried
Freshly ground black pepper
1 green pepper
3 tablespoons natural yogurt

1. Scrub the carrots and grate coarsely. Place in a bowl with the chervil and season with freshly ground black pepper.

2. De-seed and finely chop the green pepper and add to the bowl with the natural yogurt. Toss together thoroughly and serve.

Creamy Carrot Purée

(Serves 4. Supplies only a trace of fat and 70 calories per portion.)

This combination of carrots and swede is a favourite. Use skimmed milk rather than full fat milk and butter to work the cooked vegetables to a soft purée. Season generously.

Imperial (Metric)
2 lb (900g) swede
¾ lb (325g) carrots
Bay leaf
Skimmed milk to mix
Freshly ground black pepper

1. Peel the swede and dice roughly. Scrub the carrots and chop.

2. Place both in a large pan and add enough water to come half-way up the pan. Add the bay leaf. Cover, bring to the boil then reduce heat to a simmer. Cook for 40 minutes or until both the carrot and swede are really soft.

3. Drain the vegetables and remove the bay leaf. Mash with enough milk to give a soft purée. Season generously with freshly ground black pepper. Reheat gently and serve.

Braised Celery

(Serves 4. Supplies only a trace of fat and 70 calories per portion.)

Celery has become a popular ingredient in crunchy salads, but the vegetable is also good served hot. This recipe mixes carrots with celery and a good stock.

Imperial (Metric)
Head of celery
¾ lb (325g) carrots
Bay leaf
¾ pint (450ml) vegetable stock
Freshly ground black pepper

1. Scrub the celery and cut into lengths 3 inches (7.5cm) long.

2. Scrub the carrots and cut into long strips. Place both in a casserole with the bay leaf and stock. Cover tightly. Bake for 30 minutes in the centre of a pre-heated oven at 400°F/200°C (Gas Mark 6). Season and serve at once.

Low-Fat Ratatouille

(Serves 4. Supplies 1.3g fat and 70 calories per portion.)

Use less olive oil than normal, making up the difference with well-flavoured vegetable stock. This recipe freezes well so is a good way of using up a glut of courgettes from the garden.

Imperial (Metric)
½ lb (225g) aubergine
6 oz (175g) onion
3 cloves garlic
1 teaspoon olive oil
2 frozen cubes of stock
1 teaspoon dried basil *or* 2 teaspoons fresh
15 oz (425g) can tomatoes *or* 1 lb (450g) fresh, skinned
¾ lb (325g) courgettes, sliced
1 large green pepper, de-seeded and chopped
4 oz (100g) button mushrooms
Freshly ground black pepper

1. Dice the aubergine into ½-inch (1cm) cubes. Finely chop the onion and crush the garlic.

2. Heat the oil and frozen stock and then cook the aubergine, onion and garlic over a low heat for 5 minutes. Stir in the basil and cook for 1 minute more.

3. Add the tomatoes, courgettes, green pepper and mushrooms. Bring to the boil then reduce heat and let it simmer gently for 30 minutes. Season and either serve hot or let it cool completely and serve chilled.

Courgette and Tomato Salad

(Serves 4. Supplies 4.5g fat and 60 calories per portion.)

Imperial (Metric)
10 oz (275g) courgettes
1 clove garlic, crushed
1 tablespoon olive oil
Juice of ½ lemon
4 tomatoes
2 tablespoons chopped parsley

1. Wipe the courgettes and cut into slices approximately ⅜-inch (1cm) thick.

2. Steam lightly or plunge into boiling water and cook for 2 minutes. Drain and immediately toss in a bowl with the garlic, oil and lemon juice. Season with freshly ground black pepper.

3. Slice the tomatoes and add to the bowl with the parsley. Set aside to bring out the flavours before serving.

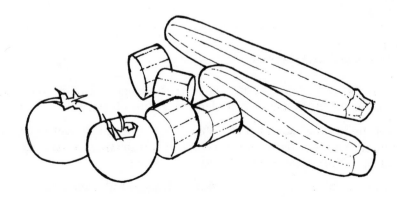

Cucumber Cooler

(Serves 4. Supplies less than 1g fat and 25 calories per portion.)

This refreshing salad goes well with curries but can be served as a simple side salad with a variety of summer dishes too.

Imperial (Metric)
4-inch (10cm) piece of cucumber
4 oz (100g) seedless white grapes
4 tablespoons natural yogurt
2 teaspoons chopped chives
Freshly ground black pepper

1. Finely dice the cucumber. Wash the grapes and halve. Mix in a bowl.

2. Pour over the yogurt, add the chives and season with freshly ground black pepper. Toss together thoroughly and chill before serving.

Spicy Mushrooms

(Serves 4. Supplies 1.6g fat and 100 calories each.)

An excellent accompaniment to Prawn and Courgette Curry (page 69). *Illustrated opposite page 81.*

Imperial (Metric)
4 cloves garlic
½-inch (1cm) cube ginger
4 tablespoons water
1 teaspoon olive oil
¾ lb (325g) button mushrooms, halved
1 teaspoon lemon juice
Freshly ground black pepper

1. Crush the garlic cloves. Peel and grate the ginger. Place in the goblet of a liquidizer with the water and blend to a smooth paste.

2. Heat the oil in a saucepan and stir in the garlic and ginger paste. Heat for 1 minute then stir in the mushrooms. Lower heat and simmer for 20 minutes, adding a little more water if needed.

3. Stir in the lemon juice, season with freshly ground black pepper and serve.

Savoy Stir-Fry

(Serves 4. Supplies only a trace of fat and 20 calories per portion.)

Savoy cabbage with its dark, crinkly leaves makes a good contrast to beanshoots in this quick and easy dish.

Imperial (Metric)
¾ lb (325g) Savoy cabbage
4 frozen cubes of stock
1 tablespoon soya sauce
1 teaspoon tomato purée
2 handsful beanshoots
2 spring onions, chopped
Freshly ground black pepper

1. Wash the cabbage and shred finely.

2. In a wok or a large, heavy-based frying pan heat the stock and soya sauce. Add the shredded cabbage and, stirring frequently, cook over a high heat for 3 minutes.

3. Stir in the tomato purée and beanshoots and mix in thoroughly. Add the spring onions and cook for a further 2-3 minutes. Season with freshly ground black pepper and serve at once.

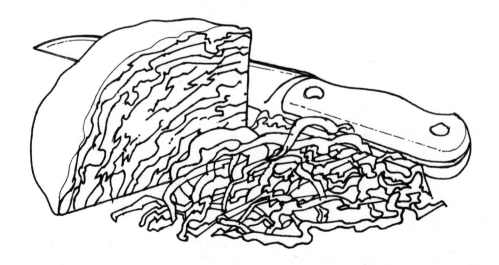

Red Cabbage Braise

(Serves 4. Supplies 1g fat and 80 calories per portion.)

A tangy way of serving red cabbage.

Imperial (Metric)
1 medium red cabbage
1 large onion
1 teaspoon sunflower oil
2 frozen cubes vegetable stock
2 eating apples, chopped
1 green pepper, chopped
2 oz (50g) sultanas
2 tablespoons cider vinegar
1 tablespoon vegetable stock or water
Freshly ground black pepper

1. Wash the cabbage and shred finely. Finely chop the onion.

2. Heat the oil and stock in a pan and stir in the onion. Cook for 2 minutes.

3. Stir in the shredded cabbage, chopped apple and pepper, sultanas, vinegar and stock. Simmer for 35 minutes over a low heat. Season and serve at once.

Red Cabbage Crunch

(Serves 4. Supplies 1g fat and 50 calories per portion.)

Makes a colourful change from white cabbage in salads.

Imperial (Metric)
4 sticks celery
1 leek
2 Granny Smith's apples
Juice of 1 lemon
½ lb (225g) red cabbage
2 oz (50g) low-fat soft cheese
1 tablespoon natural yogurt
½ teaspoon dill seeds
Freshly ground black pepper
1 green pepper, to garnish

Opposite: From the top: Pasta with Mushroom and Pepper Sauce (page 56); Hot Chilli Beans (page 109); Courgette and Nut Loaf (page 100).

1. Chop the celery finely. Trim away the coarse green leaves and roots from the leek and slice thinly. Mix together.

2. Core and dice the apples and mix with the lemon juice. Shred the red cabbage and mix with the apple. Then stir in the celery and leek mixture and toss together thoroughly.

3. Mix the soft cheese with the yogurt, dill seeds and freshly ground black pepper and pour over the salad. Toss thoroughly.

4. De-seed the pepper and cut into rings. Garnish the salad with the pepper rings and serve.

Potato and Onion Salad

(Serves 4 as a side dish. Supplies less than 1g fat and 90 calories per portion.)

Imperial (Metric)
¾ lb (325g) potatoes
Sprig of mint
4 spring onions
¾-inch (2cm) piece of cucumber
4 tablespoons natural yogurt
¼ teaspoon dill seeds
Freshly ground black pepper

1. Scrub the potatoes and cut into 2-inch (5cm) pieces. Place in a pan with the mint and cover with cold water. Bring to the boil, reduce heat and simmer for 20 minutes or until the potatoes are just soft.

2. While the potatoes are cooking trim the spring onions and chop. Dice the cucumber finely and mix with the yogurt, dill seeds and freshly ground black pepper in a bowl.

3. When the potatoes are cooked, drain and dice finely. Add to the dressing and toss thoroughly. Leave to cool before serving.

Opposite: Give your dinner party an Eastern flavour with Spicy Mushrooms (page 78); Spiced Rice (page 71); Cauliflower with Cumin and Coriander (page 68); Prawn and Courgette Curry (page 69).

Watercress and Carrot Salad

(Serves 4. Supplies 1g fat and 30 calories per portion.)

Orange is a traditional accompaniment to watercress — here it is added as juice to give an unusual dressing.

Imperial (Metric)
Bunch of watercress
½ lb (225g) carrots
1 teaspoon sunflower oil
1 tablespoon fresh orange juice
1 spring onion, chopped

1. Wash the watercress and trim any yellow leaves. Place in a bowl.

2. Scrub the carrots and grate coarsely. Add to the watercress and mix in thoroughly.

3. In a screw-top jar shake together the oil, orange juice and chopped onion. Pour over the watercress and carrot and serve.

Casseroled Potatoes

(Serves 4. Supplies 0.2g fat and 150 calories per portion.)

Imperial (Metric)
1½ lb (675g) potatoes
2 oz (50g) onion
8 fl oz (240ml) skimmed milk
Bay leaf
Freshly ground black pepper
3 tablespoons fresh chopped parsley

1. Scrub the potatoes and slice very thinly.

2. Peel the onion. Cut in half and slice thinly into semi-circles.

3. Light the oven 375°F/190°C (Gas Mark 5). Brush a shallow ovenproof dish with a little oil. Arrange the potato and onion slices neatly in the dish, place the bay leaf in the centre and season liberally with freshly ground black pepper.

4. Pour over the milk and cover tightly with aluminium foil. Bake for 45-50 minutes until the potatoes are soft. Serve sprinkled with chopped parsley.

Spinach and Mushroom Salad

(Serves 4. Supplies 2.7g fat and 45 calories per portion.)

Dark and nutritious spinach is good raw as well as lightly cooked. Mushrooms make a good contrast in colour and texture.

Imperial (Metric)
½ lb (225g) spinach
4 oz (100g) mushrooms
1 dessertspoon sunflower oil
Juice of ½ lemon
Freshly ground black pepper
½ teaspoon fresh chopped thyme *or* ¼ teaspoon dried

1. Wash the spinach thoroughly and trim away any coarse stems or yellow leaves. Shred into ½-inch (1cm) strips.

2. Wipe the mushrooms and slice thinly. Mix with the spinach.

3. In a screw-top jar shake together the oil, lemon juice, freshly ground black pepper and thyme. Pour over spinach and mushrooms and toss thoroughly.

7.

HOME BAKING

It's difficult to visualize tea-time treats without fat. By their very nature cakes and biscuits are high in fat and sugar, two undesirable ingredients in a healthy diet. Try to cut down on sweet foods like these which serve little purpose other than supplying extra calories and satisfying our sweet tooth. But for occasional treats here are some recipes using wholemeal flour which supplies extra fibre, vitamins and minerals missing from refined white flour. They are also low in fat, made by drastically cutting down the amount of margarine or butter added during mixing and keeping an eye on the amount of sugar used too! Honey is a good alternative to sugar as it has a distinctive taste, adds a deep golden colour to baked goodies and is more concentrated in sweetness, so weight for weight, less is required for the same level of sweetness.

Cutting down on fat in cakes poses several problems; fat contributes to the risen structure of a cake, to its soft texture and to its keeping qualities. These cakes depend on different ingredients for their lightness but will not keep fresh for longer than a day or two — but with hungry mouths around this is never a problem!

Biscuits lack crispness when made without fat; lowest in fat and less sweet than most are digestives. The recipe in this chapter is simple and economical and the biscuits will keep fresh for several days if kept in an air-tight container.

Finally there is a foolproof recipe for wholemeal bread. Quicker than many recipes, it produces a light well-risen wholemeal loaf that is cheaper and tastier than shop-bought bread.

Banana Cake

(Cuts into 10 slices. Supplies 0.4g fat and 100 calories each.)

A light, moist cake. Eat within two days and keep wrapped in foil.

Imperial (Metric)
4 oz (100g) carrots
2 oz (50g) dates
3 tablespoons clear honey
1 banana, mashed
6 oz (175g) wholemeal flour
1½ teaspoons baking powder
¼ teaspoon cinnamon
¼ pint (150ml) skimmed milk
2 free-range egg whites

1. Scrub the carrots and grate finely. Chop the dates finely. Lightly grease a 2 lb loaf tin and dust with wholemeal flour.

2. Place the honey in a large mixing bowl. Add the banana and beat together well. Stir in the carrots and dates. Sieve in the flour, baking powder and cinnamon and then add the bran remaining in the sieve.

3. Add the milk and mix to a batter. Stiffly whisk the egg whites and fold into the mixture. Pour into the prepared tin and smooth over top.

4. Bake in the centre of a pre-heated oven at 325°F/170°C (Gas Mark 3) for 35-40 minutes until golden brown and just firm to the touch. Cool slightly in the tin, then turn out and finish cooling on a wire cooling rack.

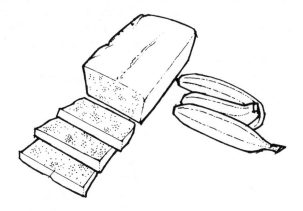

Fruity Fingers

(Makes 10. Supplies 0.6g fat and 110 calories each.)

A moist, slightly heavy texture but with a rich fruity flavour. Ideal for packed lunches.

Imperial (Metric)
½ lb (225g) cooking apples
3 oz (75g) wholemeal flour
½ teaspoon baking powder
½ teaspoon mixed spice
¼ teaspoon ground cinnamon
2 oz (50g) rolled oats
4 oz (100g) sultanas
2 oz (50g) raisins
2 oz (50g) currants
¼ pint (150ml) skimmed milk
1 free-range egg white

1. Light the oven 350°F/180°C (Gas Mark 4). Lightly grease a shallow 8-inch (20cm) square cake tin and dust with flour.

2. Peel, core and slice the cooking apples. Place in a saucepan with a little water. Cook gently over a low heat until soft and pulpy. Beat till smooth.

3. Sieve the flour with the baking powder and spices into a mixing bowl, add the bran remaining in the sieve. Stir in the rolled oats, sultanas, raisins and currants.

4. Pour in the apple purée and skimmed milk and beat thoroughly. Whisk the egg white until stiff and fold into the mixture. Pour into the prepared tin and bake in the centre of the oven for 35-40 minutes until golden brown and firm to the touch. Leave to cool in the tin on a wire rack before removing and cutting into fingers.

Swiss Roll

(Cuts into 8 pieces. Supplies 11.5g fat and 65 calories each.)

A nice light mixture which can be varied. Fill with a jam made without added sugar for a fruity flavour.

Imperial (Metric)
2 free-range eggs
1 free-range egg white
3 tablespoons clear honey
3 oz (75g) wholemeal flour
3 tablespoons no-added sugar jam

1. Light the oven 425°F/220°C (Gas Mark 7). Grease and line a swiss roll tin with greaseproof paper.

2. Place the eggs and extra egg white in a large bowl with the honey. Whisk together until the mixture is pale, thick and smooth. If using a hand whisk place the bowl over a pan of hot water as this will speed up the whisking process. The mixture is ready when the letter W can be trailed in the mixture, with first stroke still visible when you make the last.

3. Sieve in the flour and fold in gently but thoroughly with a metal spoon. Pour into the prepared tin and bake in the pre-heated oven for 8-10 minutes until the mixture springs back when touched and has shrunk away from the sides of the tin.

4. Quickly turn the cake out of the tin onto a sheet of greaseproof paper. Peel back the paper used to line the tin and spread jam over the cake. Trim off ¼-inch all round to neaten the edges of the cake. Make a small cut ½-inch away from the edge nearest to you, and roll up from there using the greaseproof paper to roll the sponge tightly. Leave to cool on a wire rack before serving.

Note: Vary this mixture by adding either 1 teaspoon decaffeinated coffee mixed with 1 teaspoon water *or* substitute ½ oz (13g) flour with carob powder. Fill with low-fat soft cheese, if liked, for a change.

Bara Brith

(Cuts into 10 slices. Supplies 2.5g fat and 125 calories each.)

Rather than relying on traditional cakes for tea-time treats use recipes which have a lower proportion of fat and are free or very low in egg content. This tea bread doesn't need butter to taste good; if liked spread with a little low-sugar fruit jam.

Imperial (Metric)
½ lb (225g) wholemeal flour
1 oz (25g) soft vegetable margarine, high in PUFA
1 teaspoon mixed spice
¼ teaspoon ground nutmeg
2 oz (50g) sultanas
3 oz (75g) raisins
Grated rind of 1 lemon
6 fl oz (180ml) skimmed milk
½ oz (13g) fresh yeast
1 teaspoon clear honey
1 teaspoon clear honey mixed with 1 teaspoon boiling water to glaze

1. Sieve the flour into a mixing bowl and add the bran remaining in the sieve. Rub in the vegetable margarine until mixture resembles fine breadcrumbs.

2. Stir in the spices, fruits and grated lemon rind.

3. Heat the milk until it is just warm to the touch and stir in the yeast and honey. Let the yeast dissolve before pouring onto the dry ingredients.

4. Mix together to form a soft dough and then turn out onto a lightly floured surface and knead until the dough is soft and smooth. Place in a bowl, covered, and leave to prove in a warm place (about 1-1¼ hours).

5. Knead dough lightly and gently pull into an oblong three times as wide as a 1 lb loaf tin. Fold the dough into three and drop into the greased tin. Cover and leave in a warm place for 20-25 minutes until doubled in size. Light the oven 450°F/230°C (Gas Mark 8).

6. Glaze with a little skimmed milk and bake for 25 minutes. Test loaf by turning it out of the tin. If it sounds hollow when tapped it is ready. Brush with the honey and water glaze and leave to cool on a wire cooling rack.

Digestive Biscuits

(Makes 20. Supplies 2.3g fat and 45 calories each.)

Many biscuits are very high in fat. This simple recipe has a relatively small amount of fat, and rather than being saturated as is the case with most commercial brands, uses a margarine high in polyunsaturated fatty acids.

Imperial (Metric)
3½ oz (88g) wholemeal flour
1½ oz (38g) fine oatmeal
½ teaspoon baking powder
Pinch of sea salt
2 oz (50g) soft vegetable margarine
1 tablespoon Muscovado sugar
2-3 tablespoons skimmed milk to mix

1. Light the oven 350°F/180°C (Gas Mark 4). Lightly grease two baking trays.

2. Sieve the flour, oatmeal, baking powder and salt into a mixing bowl and add the bran remaining in the sieve. Rub the margarine into the mixture until it resembles fine breadcrumbs.

3. Stir in the sugar and mix in the milk with the blade of a knife. Bring together with the fingers and knead lightly.

4. Roll out dough on a lightly floured surface to ⅛-inch (3mm) thickness. Stamp out rounds using a 3-inch (7.5cm) cutter.

5. Place rounds on baking trays and prick with a fork. Bake in the centre of the oven for 15 minutes until just turning brown at the edges. Transfer to wire cooling racks to cool.

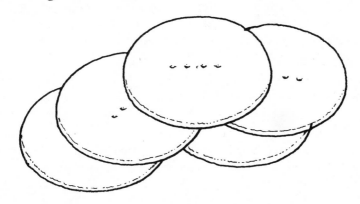

Wholemeal Bread

(This quantity of bread dough contains 2330 calories and around 34g fat. A bread roll will therefore supply 116 calories and 1.7g fat.)

This basic recipe for wholemeal bread is time-saving because it uses vitamin C to cut down on the time required to prove the dough. The result is a light loaf; the dough can be used to bake individual rolls, or as a base for pizzas. *Illustrated opposite page 48.*

Imperial (Metric)

Use Mark 4 5 on 4th shelf down (mid)

1½ lb (675g) wholemeal flour
1 teaspoon sea salt
1 oz (25g) soft vegetable margarine high in PUFA
1 oz (25g) fresh yeast
25mg vitamin C tablet
15 fl oz (450ml) tepid water
Skimmed milk to glaze

1. Mix the flour with the salt and rub in the margarine. Crumble the yeast into the water and stir in the crushed vitamin C tablet. Mix well and pour onto flour.

2. Draw together the flour and liquid with the fingers until it forms a dough.

3. Turn dough out onto a lightly floured surface and knead for 10 minutes, adding more flour if required, to give a smooth and soft dough. Cover and leave to rest for 10 minutes.

4. While the dough is resting, lightly grease two 1 lb loaf tins. Light the oven 450°F/230°C (Gas Mark 8).

5. Divide the dough into two. Shape one half into an oblong, three times the width of the tin. Fold over and with the seam underneath, place the dough in a tin. Repeat with remaining dough. Cover and leave to prove in a warm place until double in size. This takes around 25-35 minutes. The dough should spring back when touched with the fingertip.

6. Brush with skimmed milk and bake at the top of the oven for 25-30 minutes. Test by tipping the loaf out of the tin and tapping the underneath. If it sounds hollow then the loaf is ready. Remove from the tins and leave to cool on wire cooling racks.

Note: To make bread rolls divide the dough into 20 even-sized pieces. Shape each into a roll, place them spaced apart on greased baking trays and cover and leave to prove in a warm place for 20-25 minutes. Glaze and bake for 15-20 minutes.

8.

ENTERTAINING IDEAS

Most cooks take great pleasure in offering friends and relatives the best dishes in their culinary repertoire. And usually that means reaching for the cream and butter to concoct those extra-rich dishes reserved for special occasions. But if you are trying to limit the fat content of your diet there is no reason why you should suddenly undo all the good work when entertaining. There are many delicious dishes which can be made with small amounts of added fat which are good enough to grace any dining table.

The golden rule, as always, is to start with basic ingredients which are low in fat and to avoid adding extra fat when cooking and serving. That doesn't mean food has to be plain and simple; on the contrary there are many ways of transforming low-fat foods into impressive dishes. Take extra trouble in presenting each dish attractively to delight the eye as well as the palate.

When eating out it is less easy to avoid eating too much — it is difficult to know just how dishes have been cooked. The safest bet is to choose plainly cooked food — grilled rather than fried food, simple vegetables rather than elaborate, and fresh fruit, sorbets and fruit salads, all of which will be healthier alternatives to those cream-laden desserts on the groaning sweet trolley!

In this chapter there are 10 menus to help you keep down the fat content of food when catering for others. Some are formal, others less so. As always, remember to balance each course so that the complete meal offers contrasting colours, flavours and textures.

MENU 1

Mushrooms Casseroled with Red Wine
Tropical Chicken with boiled rice
Raspberry Whip

Mushrooms Casseroled with Red Wine

(Serves 4. Supplies 1.4g fat and 80 calories per portion.)

Imperial (Metric)
½ lb (225g) button mushrooms
3 oz (75g) onion
2 cloves garlic
½ red pepper
1 teaspoon olive oil
2 glasses red wine
Bay leaf
¼ teaspoon dried thyme
Freshly ground black pepper

1. Wipe the mushrooms and chop finely. Finely chop the onion and crush the garlic. De-seed and finely chop the red pepper.

2. Place the oil in a saucepan and stir in the onion and garlic. Cook gently for 2 minutes. Now add the chopped mushrooms and cook for a further minute.

3. Pour in the red wine, add the red pepper, bay leaf and thyme. Cover and simmer for 40 minutes. Season with freshly ground black pepper and serve with wholemeal bread.

Tropical Chicken

(Serves 4. Supplies 9g fat and 240 calories per portion.)

A hint of curry spices and a touch of sweetness give this chicken dish a special flavour.

Imperial (Metric)
½ lb (225g) carrots
1 large onion
2 sticks celery
2 cloves garlic
1 teaspoon sunflower oil
2 frozen cubes of vegetable stock
½ teaspoon ground coriander
½ teaspoon ground cumin
1 lb (450g) boned and skinned chicken, cut into bite-sized pieces
1 pint (600ml) vegetable or chicken stock
8 fl oz (240ml) pineapple juice
3 tablespoons tomato purée
3 oz (75g) dried apricots, chopped
4 tablespoons sweetcorn kernels
2 bay leaves
1 green pepper
Cornflour to thicken
1 banana, sliced
Freshly ground black pepper

1. Scrub the carrots and cut into fine matchsticks, 1-inch (2.5cm) long. Finely chop the onion and celery and crush the garlic.

2. Heat the oil and frozen stock then lower heat and add the prepared vegetables. Cook gently for 3 minutes without browning. Stir in the coriander and cumin and cook for 1 minute.

3. Add the chicken and toss in the mixture so that it takes up some of the colour. Add the stock, pineapple juice, tomato purée, chopped apricots, sweetcorn and bay leaves. Bring to the boil, cover and reduce heat. Simmer for 1 hour.

4. De-seed and chop the pepper and add to the pan. If the liquid needs thickening mix a little cornflour with cold water and stir into the pan; let it boil then lower heat, stir in sliced banana and season. Serve at once with boiled rice.

Raspberry Whip

(Serves 4. Supplies 0.2g fat and 55 calories per portion.)

A tangy, super smooth dessert.

Imperial (Metric)
¾ lb (325g) raspberries
8 fl oz (240ml) natural yogurt
1 dessertspoon clear honey
2 free-range egg whites

1. Wash the raspberries. Place in the goblet of a liquidizer with the yogurt and honey and blend until smooth.

2. Pour into a bowl. Stiffly whisk the egg whites and using a metal spoon fold into the raspberry mixture. Pour into serving glasses and chill.

MENU 2

Avocado and Orange Salad
Rich Vegetable Casserole with
baked potatoes or rice
Fruit Sorbet

Avocado and Orange Salad

(Serves 4. Supplies 1.4g fat and 170 calories per portion.)

Arranged on individual plates this looks attractive and appetizing but remember that avocados have a very high natural fat content — use sparingly.

Imperial (Metric)
2 avocados
2 oranges
4 oz (100g) low-fat soft cheese
1-inch (2.5cm) piece cucumber
Freshly ground black pepper
1 tablespoon chopped chives *or* ½ teaspoon dill seeds

1. Halve the avocados and remove the stone from each. Cut the flesh into slices.

2. Peel the oranges and remove any pith. Arrange segments with avocado slices on four small plates, leaving space in the centre for the dressing.

3. Place the cheese in a bowl. Grate the cucumber and mix with the cheese. Season with freshly ground black pepper and add the chives or dill seeds. Divide between four plates and arrange in the centre of the avocado and orange pieces. Serve at once.

Rich Vegetable Casserole
Illustrated opposite page 96.

(Serves 4. Supplies under 1g fat and 140 calories per portion.)

Imperial (Metric)
4 oz (100g) onion
2 sticks celery
6 oz (175g) carrots
½ pint (300ml) vegetable stock
1 small sized cauliflower
1 small aubergine
½ lb (225g) canned red kidney beans, drained
½ pint (300ml) tomato juice
½ pint (300ml) red wine
2 bay leaves
Sprig of fresh thyme *or* ½ teaspoon dried
4 oz (100g) green cabbage, shredded
1 dessertspoon cornflour to thicken
Freshly ground black pepper

1. Peel and finely chop the onion. Chop the celery. Scrub the carrots and cut into rings.

2. Put 3 tablespoons vegetable stock in a large saucepan and sauté the onion, celery and carrots in it. Cook gently for 3 minutes.

3. Meanwhile, divide the cauliflower into florets and slice the aubergine. Add both to the pan with remaining stock, red kidney beans, tomato juice, red wine and herbs. Bring to the boil then simmer gently for 15 minutes.

4. Stir in the shredded cabbage and cook for a further 4 minutes. Thicken the mixture with cornflour mixed with a little cold water. Season generously and serve at once with baked potatoes or rice.

Fruit Sorbet

Sorbets are light, refreshing and low in calories. Rather than using refined white sugar this recipe is based on fruit sugar (fructose). Fructose is nature's sweetest sugar and so less needs to be used in a recipe to give the same amount of sweetness. Most sugars in this book are of the raw cane variety but imagine a delicate sorbet marred with brown sugar! Fructose is available from health food stores and some chemists. Purées of almost any fruit can be converted into sorbets; try serving more tangy fruit sorbets as a second course in an impressive four course meal. Grapefruit, orange and lemon are ideal for this. Serve a scoop of two contrasting sorbets together; pale pink raspberry for example with cool green melon. This basic recipe is enough for 4 people.

Imperial (Metric)
2 oz (50g) fructose
¼ pint (150ml) cold water
1 lb (450g) soft fruit of your choice
2 free-range egg whites

1. Place the fructose and water in a small pan and heat gently until the sugar has dissolved. Boil for one minute and remove from heat. Leave to cool.

2. Prepare your chosen fruit; peel, chop and purée (cooking if required). Sieve to remove any pips or unwanted skins.

3. Place the fructose syrup and the fruit purée in a blender goblet and blend until smooth.

4. Pour into a shallow polythene container and freeze for 3-4 hours until just mushy.

5. Beat with a fork to break up any ice crystals. Stiffly whisk the egg whites and fold into the fruit mixture with a metal spoon. Return to the freezer and freeze until firm (about 3 hours). Spoon or scoop into individual serving glasses.

Opposite: For a warming winter's meal try Rich Vegetable Casserole (page 95).

```
┌─────────────────────────────────────────────┐
│                  MENU 3                        │
│                                                │
│       Italian Tomato and Courgette Soup        │
│            with wholemeal bread                │
│          Baked Trout, with potatoes            │
│            and green vegetables                │
│          Melon and Grape Dessert               │
└─────────────────────────────────────────────┘
```

Italian Tomato and Courgette Soup

(Serves 4. Supplies 1.2g fat and 40 calories per portion.)

Use a small amount of good quality olive oil to give this light soup a rich flavour.

Imperial (Metric)
3 oz (75g) onion
2 cloves garlic
1 teaspoon olive oil
2 frozen cubes of vegetable stock
¾ teaspoon dried marjoram or basil or 1½ teaspoons chopped fresh
Bay leaf
1 lb (450g) fresh tomatoes, skinned and chopped or 15 oz (425g) tin,
    chopped
12 fl oz (360ml) vegetable stock
6 oz (175g) courgettes
4 tablespoons chopped fresh parsley
Freshly ground black pepper

1. Finely chop the onion and crush the garlic. Sauté together in the oil and frozen
    stock cubes for 1 minute.

2. Add the marjoram or basil plus the tomatoes and stock and bring to the boil.
    Reduce heat and simmer for 20 minutes.

3. Wipe the courgettes and cut into matchsticks each 1-inch (2.5cm) long. Add
    to the soup and cook for a further 5 minutes. Add the parsley and season
    with the pepper. Serve at once.

Opposite: Tempt your dinner guests with this delightful Hazelnut and Banana Gâteau
(page 114).

98

Baked Trout

(Serves 4. Supplies 10g of fat and 320 calories per portion.)

Trout contains less fat than oily fish and slightly more than white fish like cod and plaice. Its rich flavour is offset by lemon juice in this simple and speedy recipe. Keep the heads on for cooking as the eyes help to indicate when the fish is cooked — when they turn opaque the fish is ready.

Imperial (Metric)
4 trout, about ½ lb (225g) each
Juice of 1 lemon
2 tablespoons wholemeal flour
Freshly ground black pepper

1. Ask the fishmonger to clean the trout. Wash each well removing any blood that remains inside. Pat dry with a clean cloth. Light the oven 450°F/230°C (Gas Mark 8) and let it heat up fully.

2. Brush the insides of each trout with lemon juice and lightly brush the outside skin too. Place the flour on a plate and season with the pepper. Toss each trout in the flour.

3. Lay a sheet of foil on a baking tray and arrange the trout on top. When the oven has heated up place the tray on the top shelf and bake for 7 minutes. Turn the trout and return to oven for a further 2 minutes, basting with the juices which will run from the fish. Serve at once with baked potatoes and a green vegetable or side salad.

Melon and Grape Dessert

(Serves 4. Supplies a trace of fat and 90 calories per portion.)

Choose the delicately coloured flesh of the Galia melon for this pretty dessert.

Imperial (Metric)
1 small Galia melon
4 nectarines
4 apricots
6 oz (175g) small seedless white grapes
Juice of 2 oranges or ¼ pint (150ml) fresh orange juice
1 tablespoon Cointreau (optional)

1. Cut the melon into quarters and remove the seeds. Either remove the flesh using a melon scoop or cut into bite-sized pieces.

2. Halve the nectarines and remove the stones; dice the flesh. Repeat with the apricots.

3. Mix all together in a bowl and add the grapes, orange juice and Cointreau if using. Cover and chill for 30 minutes to let the flavours mingle. Serve with natural yogurt.

MENU 4

Grilled Grapefruit
Courgette and Nut Loaf with
potatoes and a side salad
Jellied Fruit Cups with yogurt

Grilled Grapefruit

(Serves 4. Supplies a trace of fat and 105 calories per portion.)

Imperial (Metric)
2 grapefruit
4 tablespoons dry sherry
4 tablespoons Demerara sugar

1. Cut the grapefruit in half and cut in between the segments using a small sharp knife. Cut round the outside, slipping the knife under the central core. Remove any pips.

2. Sprinkle one tablespoon dry sherry and one tablespoon sugar on top of each.

3. Heat the grill to red hot. Place the prepared grapefruit underneath and grill until the sugar caramelizes lightly and serve at once.

Courgette and Nut Loaf
Illustrated opposite page 80.

(Serves 4. Supplies 11g fat and 230 calories per portion.)

Imperial (Metric)
4 oz (100g) onion
A little oil
3 sticks celery
6 oz (175g) carrots
6 oz (175g) courgettes
6 oz (175g) wholemeal breadcrumbs
2 oz (50g) ground peanuts
2½ oz (63g) ground hazelnuts
½ teaspoon rosemary, chopped
½ teaspoon dried thyme
Freshly ground black pepper
Free-range egg
2 tablespoons vegetable stock
1 tablespoon tomato purée

1. Lightly grease a 2 lb loaf tin. Light the oven 375°F/190°C (Gas Mark 5).

2. Finely chop the onion and cook over a low heat in the oil for 2 minutes. Place in a large mixing bowl.

3. Finely chop the celery, scrub and grate the carrots and grate the courgettes. Add to the bowl.

4. Stir in the breadcrumbs, peanuts and hazelnuts, rosemary and thyme. Mix together thoroughly. Bind the mixture with the egg, stock and tomato purée. Put into tin and smooth top. Cover with foil and bake at the top of the oven for 30 minutes. Remove foil and continue cooking a further 10 minutes without the foil.

5. Turn out and serve sliced, either hot or cold. The mixture could also be baked in a ring mould and served with a salad in the centre.

Jellied Fruit Cups

(Serves 4. Supplies only a trace of fat and 55 calories per portion.)

Choose good quality fruit for this simple dessert and arrange attractively.

Imperial (Metric)
Small bunch black grapes
Small honeydew melon
1 peach *or* 1 orange
1 pint (600ml) white grape juice or apple juice
½ oz (13g) gelatine *or* equivalent of vegetarian setting agent

1. Wash the fruit well. Halve and de-seed the grapes. Cut the melon in two, scoop out seeds and remove flesh with a melon ball cutter. Cut the peach or orange flesh into small dice. Arrange attractively in four individual glass serving dishes.

2. Heat the fruit juice and dissolve the gelatine or setting agent in it. Pour over fruit gently so as not to disturb the pattern. Leave to set in the fridge before serving with natural yogurt.

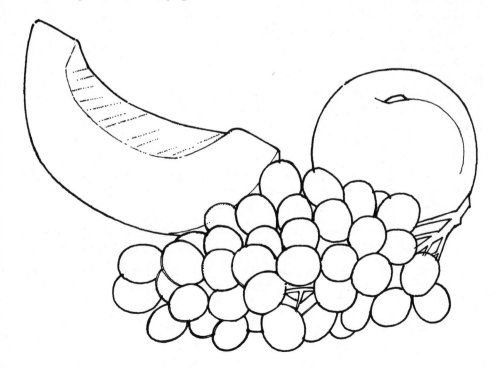

```
┌─────────────────────────────────────────────┐
│                                               │
│                   MENU 5                      │
│                                               │
│              Beans à la Grecque               │
│          Mushroom Stuffed Plaice with         │
│         potatoes and a green vegetable        │
│           Fresh Fruit Salad with yogurt       │
│                                               │
└─────────────────────────────────────────────┘
```

Beans à la Grecque

(Serves 4. Supplies only a trace of fat and 25 calories per portion.)

Mushrooms, courgettes and cauliflower florets can also be served in this way to make a chilled starter.

Imperial (Metric)
2 cloves garlic
2 ripe tomatoes
1 tablespoon tomato purée
2 tablespoons dry white wine or dry cider
4 fl oz (120ml) water
4 coriander seeds
Bay leaf
¼ teaspoon dried thyme or ½ teaspoon fresh
¼ teaspoon dried oregano or ½ teaspoon fresh
Freshly ground black pepper
¾ lb (325g) French beans

1. Peel and crush the garlic. Skin the tomatoes. Place in a saucepan with the tomato purée, wine or cider, water, coriander seeds, bay leaf, thyme and oregano. Bring to the boil and simmer for 5 minutes.

2. Meanwhile trim the beans and cut into 1-inch (2.5cm) pieces. Add to the sauce and simmer until just soft. Remove the beans and rub the sauce through a sieve.

3. Heat the sauce for 5 minutes to reduce it. Pour over beans and leave in the fridge to chill. Season with freshly ground black pepper and serve.

Mushroom Stuffed Plaice

(Serves 4. Supplies 2.7g fat and 130 calories per portion.)

Choose small plaice for this dish, as they are left whole.

Imperial (Metric)
4 small plaice
3 oz (75g) onion
3 oz (75g) button mushrooms
1 teaspoon sunflower oil
½ teaspoon dried thyme *or* 1 teaspoon fresh chopped
1 tablespoon chopped parsley
3 oz (75g) wholemeal breadcrumbs
1 tablespoon vegetable stock
Freshly ground black pepper

1. Ask the fishmonger to clean the plaice. Wash them and pat dry. Place dark
    side down on a chopping board and with a sharp knife make a cut along
    the backbone of the fish. Gently ease away the flesh either side so you are
    left with two pockets to stuff.

2. To make the stuffing, finely chop the onion and mushrooms. Sauté the onion
    in the oil gently for 2 minutes. Add the mushrooms and continue to cook
    until the juices run.

3. Place the onion and mushroom mixture in a bowl and add the remaining
    ingredients. Mix in thoroughly.

4. Stuff each plaice firmly. Arrange the fish in a shallow ovenproof dish with
    a tablespoon cold water in the base. Cover with foil and bake in the centre
    of a pre-heated oven 375°F/190°C (Gas Mark 5) for 20 minutes. Serve hot.

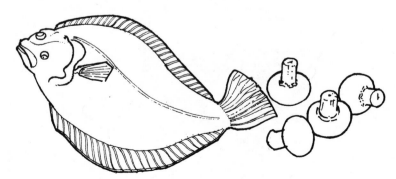

Fresh Fruit Salad

(Serves 4. Supplies only a trace of fat and around 90 calories each.)

This dessert can be served at any time of the year and is equally suitable for simple family meals and more formal dinner parties. Simply vary the fruit used and for a more exotic dish add some chopped mango, kiwifruit or papaya. Serve with yogurt rather than cream to keep down the fat content. *Illustrated opposite page 49.*

Imperial (Metric)
Small bunch grapes, white or black
2 oranges
2 peaches, nectarines or pears
½ melon
Few strawberries or raspberries if in season
3 red-skinned eating apples
Juice of 1 lemon
3 tablespoons orange juice
1 banana

1. Wash the grapes, halve and remove pips. Peel the oranges and cut into chunks, removing pith. Halve and chop the nectarines or peaches (if using pears prepare with the apples and place in lemon juice). Scoop out the melon seeds and dice flesh. Mix all the fruit in a bowl as you prepare it.

2. Core and chop the apples finely mixing with lemon juice to stop browning. Add to the bowl. Pour over orange juice and stir in well. Chill before serving and when ready to serve, slice the banana into the bowl.

MENU 6

Mango with Prawns
Chicken Provençal
with baked potatoes or rice
Apricot Fluff

Mango with Prawns

(Serves 4. Supplies 0.9g fat and 120 calories per portion.)

Imperial (Metric)
2 small mangoes
2 oz (50g) low-fat soft cheese
3 tablespoons low-fat natural yogurt
½ teaspoon ground cumin seeds
¼ teaspoon ground coriander
Pinch of cayenne pepper
Freshly ground black pepper
6 oz (175g) peeled prawns

1. Cut the mangoes in half and remove the stone. Wipe the outsides.

2. Mix together the soft cheese, yogurt, cumin, coriander and cayenne and season with freshly ground black pepper. Stir in the prawns.

3. Fill the centres of each mango half with the prawn mixture and chill until required.

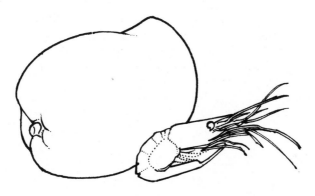

Chicken Provençal

(Serves 4. Supplies 5.8g of fat and 260 calories per portion.)

Choose skinned and boned chicken breasts for this simple dish. The addition of dry cider or wine adds extra richness to the sauce, but for a more economical dish use extra stock as a substitute.

Imperial (Metric)
4 boned chicken breasts
4 oz (100g) onion
Clove of garlic
Stick of celery
1 green pepper
4 oz (100g) button mushrooms
2×15 oz (425g) can tomatoes or 2 lb fresh tomatoes, skinned
¼ pint (150ml) vegetable stock
¼ pint (150ml) dry cider or dry white wine
1 teaspoon dried oregano or marjoram *or* 2 teaspoons fresh, chopped
6 oz (175g) courgettes
Freshly ground black pepper
2 tablespoons fresh chopped parsley

1. Wash the chicken breasts and remove the skin. Finely chop the onion and crush the garlic. Chop the celery and pepper and wipe and slice the mushrooms.

2. Put all these ingredients into a casserole dish with the chicken. Add the tomatoes (skinned if using fresh), cider or wine, stock and the oregano or marjoram. Mix in well, cover tightly and place in a pre-heated oven at 375°F/190°C (Gas Mark 5) for 1 hour.

3. Wipe and slice the courgettes into rings and add to the casserole. Continue cooking a further 20 minutes, adding a little extra vegetable stock if necessary. Season with freshly ground black pepper and sprinkle parsley on top. Serve at once.

Apricot Fluff

(Serves 4. Supplies 2.5g fat and 170 calories each.)

Dried apricots are nutritious and produce a tasty and tangy dessert when mixed with low-fat soft cheese. Try using tofu, a soya based product available from health food stores, for a change.

Imperial (Metric)
½ lb (225g) dried apricots, soaked overnight in ½ pint (300ml) water
Grated rind of 1 lemon
½-inch (1cm) piece of cinnamon
1 tablespoon clear honey
6 oz (175g) low-fat soft cheese or tofu
2 free-range egg whites
Twists of lemon to garnish

1. Place the soaked apricots with the water, lemon rind and cinnamon in a pan and cook gently for 15 minutes until soft. Remove the cinnamon and purée fruit.

2. Stir the honey and low-fat soft cheese or tofu into the apricots and blend in well.

3. Stiffly whisk the egg whites and fold into the apricot mixture. Pour into four serving glasses and decorate with a lemon twist. Chill for 30 minutes before serving.

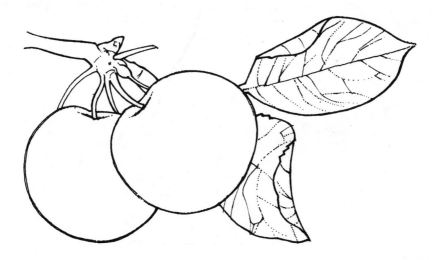

MENU 7

Spring Cocktail
Hot Chilli Beans with rice
Raisin Stuffed Apples with yogurt

Spring Cocktail

(Serves 4. Supplies a trace of fat and 20 calories per portion.)

Imperial (Metric)
½ honeydew melon
2 ripe tomatoes
3-inch (7.5cm) piece of cucumber
Juice of 1 lime
Juice of 1 small orange
1 tablespoon fresh mint

1. Cut away the flesh from the melon, discarding the seeds. Dice the flesh and place in a bowl.

2. Cut the tomatoes into small cubes and dice the cucumber. Add to the melon and pour over the lime juice and orange juice.

3. Chop the mint finely and add to the bowl. Cover and leave to marinade for at least an hour before serving in individual serving dishes.

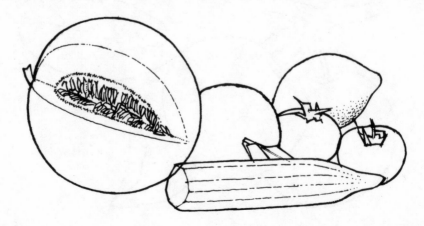

Hot Chilli Beans

(Serves 4. Supplies 1.5g fat and 210 calories per portion.)

A vegetarian alternative to a favourite supper dish. *Illustrated opposite page 80.*

Imperial (Metric)
6 oz (175g) onion
6 oz (175g) carrots
Stick of celery
3 green chillies
1 green pepper
1 red pepper
6 oz (175g) red kidney beans, soaked overnight
3 oz (175g) black kidney beans, soaked overnight
2 lbs (900g) fresh tomatoes, skinned or 2×15 oz (425g) tins
¼ pint (150ml) vegetable stock
¾ teaspoon ground cumin seeds
Freshly ground black pepper

1. Peel and finely chop the onion and carrots. Chop the celery. De-seed and very finely chop the chillies and de-seed and chop the peppers.

2. Place all the vegetables in a large saucepan and add the drained red and black kidney beans, tomatoes (skinned if using fresh), stock and cumin. Cover pan and bring to the boil. Boil for 10 minutes and then lower heat.

3. Simmer steadily for 1¾-2 hours until the beans are just tender. Check during cooking to ensure the mixture does not become too dry, and if necessary add extra stock. Season with freshly ground black pepper and serve hot with plain boiled long grain brown rice or baked potatoes and a crisp side salad.

Raisin Stuffed Apples

(Serves 4. Supplies a trace of fat and 160 calories per portion.)

An old family favourite. Serve topped with natural yogurt.

Imperial (Metric)
4 even-sized cooking apples
4 oz (100g) raisins
2 tablespoons clear honey

1. Light the oven 400°F/200°C (Gas Mark 6).

2. Wash and core the apples. Slit the skins around the middle of the apples.

3. Place the apples in a shallow ovenproof dish and place 3 tablespoons cold water in the base to stop the apples from sticking and becoming dry.

4. Carefully spoon the raisins into the apple cavities and pour honey over each. Bake in the oven for 20-30 minutes until the apples are just soft. Watch the apples carefully as cooking times vary with the type of apple used. Test by inserting the blade of a small knife into the slit skin; if the apple is soft it is ready to eat.

> **MENU 8**
>
> Savoury Peach
> Salmon Parcels with new potatoes
> and vegetables
> Poached Pears with yogurt

Savoury Stuffed Peach

(Serves 4. Supplies 1g fat and 60 calories per portion.)

This recipe is based on an idea sampled at a favourite hotel in Hope Cove, Devon.

Imperial (Metric)
4 ripe peaches
3 oz (75g) low-fat soft cheese
1 tablespoon chopped fresh chives
Generous pinch of dried thyme or teaspoon fresh chopped
Freshly ground black pepper
Sesame seeds

1. Halve the peaches and remove the stones. In a bowl mix together the low-fat soft cheese, herbs and freshly ground black pepper.

2. Fill the centre of each peach half with a little of the cheese mixture.

3. Place the peaches in a shallow heatproof dish with 2 tablespoons water in the base. Cover with aluminium foil and bake in the centre of a pre-heated oven at 400°F/200°C (Gas Mark 6) for 10 minutes. Remove foil, sprinkle sesame seeds on top and cook a further 5 minutes. Serve hot.

Salmon Parcels

(Serves 4. Supplies 20g fat and 355 calories per portion.)

Salmon can be cooked in aluminium foil to bring out the full flavour as it cooks in its own juices. A sliver of root ginger makes an interesting addition to this dish.

Imperial (Metric)
4×6 oz (175g) salmon steaks
2 tablespoons sultanas
Piece of root ginger
Freshly ground black pepper
2 tablespoons fresh chopped parsley

1. Place each salmon steak in the centre of an 8-inch (20cm) square piece of aluminium foil. Divide the sultanas equally between each portion. Peel the ginger and cut four very fine slivers. Place one in each parcel, on top of the fish. Sprinkle with freshly ground black pepper and firmly seal the foil.

2. Place on a baking sheet and bake in a pre-heated oven at 400°F/200°C (Gas Mark 6) for 20 minutes. Serve on plates and gently open the foil at the top. Sprinkle parsley inside.

Poached Pears

(Serves 4. Supplies only a trace of fat and 44 calories per portion.)

Imperial (Metric)
1 lb (450g) pears — choose firm cooking pears rather than soft eating fruit
4 cloves
½-inch (1cm) piece of cinnamon
Rind of 1 lemon, pared thinly
Water to cover
1 tablespoon clear honey

1. Wash the pears, halve and remove core. Place in a shallow dish with the cloves, cinnamon and lemon rind and just cover with water. Dribble honey over the top.

2. Cover and bake at 350°F/180°C (Gas Mark 4) for 1-1½ hours until tender. Serve hot with yogurt.

> **MENU 9: A Sunday Lunch**
>
> Pot Roast Chicken
> with casseroled potatoes
> and two vegetables
> Hazelnut and Banana Gâteau

Pot Roast Chicken

(Serves 4. Supplies 6g fat and 330 calories per portion.)

Cider is used to cook this chicken dish; place in either a casserole with a tight-fitting lid or cover tightly with foil to let the bird cook in the aromatic steam.

Imperial (Metric)
4 oz (100g) long grain brown rice
1 green pepper
3 oz (75g) raisins
1 tablespoon chives
1 tablespoon dry cider
Freshly ground black pepper
Fresh chicken, preferably free-range, weighing about 3½-4 lbs (1.6-1.8 kilos)
¼ pint (150ml) dry cider
Sprig fresh rosemary or ½ teaspoon dried
2 oz (50g) onion
Stick of celery

1. Make the stuffing. Boil the rice until just tender, drain and set aside. De-seed and finely chop the pepper. Add to the rice with the raisins, chopped chives, 1 tablespoon cider and season with freshly ground black pepper. Light the oven 375°F/190°C (Gas Mark 5).

2. Wipe the chicken and pat dry. Stuff the body cavity with the rice mixture. Place the chicken in a casserole or ovenproof dish.

3. Pour over ¼ pint (150ml) cider and place sprigs of rosemary on top of the chicken. Season lightly with freshly ground black pepper. Finely chop the onion and celery and add to the dish. Cover tightly and place in the centre of the oven to cook for 1¾-2 hours, basting every half-hour with the stock. Remove foil or lid 15 minutes from the end of cooking time. Carve, removing skin, and serve with the stock and a spoonful of stuffing.

Hazelnut and Banana Gâteau

(Serves 7. Supplies 3.8g of fat and 120 calories per portion.)

It's hard to believe this lighter than air gâteau contains no extra fat — its only drawback is the eggs it contains. Serve it on special occasions, and remember to use low-fat soft cheese or a thick set natural yogurt for the filling. *Illustrated opposite page 97.*

Imperial (Metric)
3 free-range eggs
3 oz (75g) clear honey
2½ oz (63g) wholemeal flour
½ oz (13g) ground hazelnuts
4 oz (100g) low-fat soft cheese
Juice of ½ lemon
2 bananas

1. Grease and line two 7-inch (17.5cm) sandwich cake tins. Light the oven 425°F/220°C (Gas Mark 7).

2. Place the eggs and honey in a large mixing bowl and whisk together. If beating by hand the mixture will thicken quicker if the bowl is placed over a pan of boiling water. This isn't necessary if using an electric mixer. Whisk the mixture until it is thick, pale and smooth. Test by trailing the mixture into a letter W; if when you make the last stroke the first stroke is still visible, then the mixture is ready.

3. Sieve the flour and dust the bran into the bowl with the ground hazelnuts and sieved flour. Fold in gently using a metal spoon. When thoroughly mixed in pour into the prepared tins and bake in the centre of the oven for 15-20 minutes until just firm to the touch and when the cakes have shrunk away from the sides of the tins. Place on wire cooling trays and leave to settle for one minute before carefully tipping out and leaving to cool thoroughly.

4. When the cakes are quite cold, place the low-fat soft cheese in a bowl. Add the lemon juice and the bananas. Mash together and spread half this mixture on one half of the cake, sandwich the two together and spread the remainder on top. This cake will not keep — and is best eaten really fresh so do not make too far in advance of serving time.

> **MENU 10: An Informal Barbecue Party**
>
> Smoked Mackerel Dip with crudités
> Spiced Fish Kebabs *or*
> Mixed Vegetable Kebabs
> with Spiced Mushroom Rice
> Fruity Skewers

Smoked Mackerel Dip

(Serves 4-6. Supplies 4.5g fat and 60 calories per portion.)

This easy-to-prepare dip makes a perfect starter for an informal supper; serve with crudités or strips of wholemeal toast.

Imperial (Metric)
6 oz (175g) smoked mackerel fillets
4 oz (100g) low-fat soft cheese
Juice of ½ lemon
Freshly ground black pepper
Fresh chives or parsley to garnish

1. Remove the flesh of the mackerel from the skin and take out any bones. Chop flesh roughly.

2. Mix the soft cheese with the mackerel and lemon juice and season to taste. Pound together thoroughly until the mixture is smooth and well mixed. Chill until required. Garnish with chopped chives or parsley.

Note: If serving with crudités choose from celery, carrots, cauliflower florets, red or green peppers, mushrooms, cucumber and fennel. Cut all vegetables into even pieces.

Spiced Fish Kebabs

(Serves 4. Supplies 2.3g fat and 170 calories each.)

The best fish for kebabs is monkfish, but this tends to be expensive and may not always be available. As an alternative chunky pieces of cod or haddock could be used. If liked serve a mixed vegetable kebab with these fish kebabs. Rice is the perfect accompaniment.

Imperial (Metric)
1¼ lb (550g) monkfish *or* chunky cod *or* haddock fillet
5 fl oz (150ml) natural yogurt
1 teaspoon olive oil
½ teaspoon ground coriander
½ teaspoon ground cumin seeds
⅛ teaspoon cayenne pepper
⅛ teaspoon turmeric
Freshly ground black pepper
2 onions

1. Wash the fish and cut into pieces about 1-inch (2.5cm) square. Place in a bowl.

2. Mix together the yogurt, olive oil and spices and season with pepper. Stir together and pour over the fish. Leave to marinade for 2-4 hours.

3. Peel the onions and cut into quarters. Arrange the onions and fish on skewers. Have ready a barbecue or hot grill. Cook the kebabs for 10-15 minutes, basting frequently with the marinade. Serve at once with the remaining marinade spooned over as a sauce.

Mixed Vegetable Kebabs

(Serves 4. Supplies 1.4g fat and 60 calories per portion.)

Imperial (Metric)
1 medium sized aubergine
Sea salt
¾ lb (325g) courgettes
½ lb (225g) button mushrooms
1 green pepper
2 small onions
4 medium sized tomatoes

Marinade:

Imperial (Metric)
Juice of 1 lemon
1 clove of garlic, crushed
1 teaspoon olive oil
Sprig fresh rosemary *or* ¼ teaspoon dried
Freshly ground black pepper

1. First prepare the aubergine. Cut into slices ½-inch (1cm) thick. Sprinkle with sea salt and leave for 30 minutes to draw out the bitterness. Wipe and pat dry and cut into chunks.

2. Mix together the marinade ingredients, chopping the fresh rosemary. Place in a bowl with the aubergine. Leave to marinade for 30 minutes.

3. Cut the courgettes into slices just under ½-inch (1cm) thick. Wipe the mushrooms, de-seed the pepper and cut into pieces ½-inch (1cm) square. Peel and quarter the onions and quarter the tomatoes.

4. Have ready four skewers. Starting with a piece of courgette arrange all the vegetables on the skewers. Heat the grill to red hot. Brush the kebabs with the marinade and cook for 15 minutes, turning and basting frequently. Alternatively cook over a barbecue. Serve with rice and a salad.

Spiced Mushroom Rice

(Serves 4. Supplies 0.7g fat and 200 calories per portion.)

Imperial (Metric)
2 cloves garlic
½-inch (1cm) cube root ginger
2 tablespoons water
1 small onion
½ teaspoon ground cumin
Pinch of cayenne pepper
½ lb (225g) long-grain brown rice
18 fl oz (540ml) vegetable stock
Bay leaf
6 oz (175g) mushrooms, chopped
Freshly ground black pepper

1. Crush the garlic and peel and grate the ginger. Place in a liquidizer and blend with the water until smooth.

2. Heat this paste in a saucepan and add the chopped onion. Cook for 1 minute. Stir in the cumin and cayenne pepper and cook for a further minute. Add the rice and stir to coat the grains evenly.

3. Pour in the stock, add the bay leaf and mushrooms and bring to the boil. Reduce heat and cook slowly for 25-30 minutes until all the liquid is absorbed and the rice is just tender. Do not stir rice while cooking.

4. When tender, turn off the heat and leave the pan on the ring for a further 5 minutes. Season with pepper and serve at once. This makes an ideal accompaniment to kebabs and all types of Indian dishes.

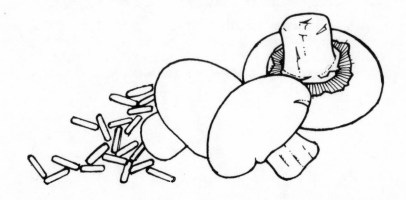

Fruity Skewers

(Serves 4. Supplies only a trace of fat and 100 calories per portion.)

A good way of finishing off a barbecue. Have ready a bowl of fruit pieces soaking in juice and ask guests to skewer their own selection and then cook them. Choose fairly firm-fleshed fruit that will not break up as it cooks.

Imperial (Metric)
1 melon
2 nectarines
Juice of 1 lemon
2 bananas
1 small pineapple or tin pineapple pieces
¼ pint (150ml) fresh orange juice
¼ -inch (0.5cm) piece of cinnamon stick
Pinch of ground ginger

1. Cut the melon into quarters, scoop out the seeds and cut the flesh into large cubes. Halve the nectarines and cut into large cubes. Peel and slice the bananas. Peel and chop the fresh pineapple.

2. Mix together in a bowl and pour over the orange juice. Add the cinnamon and ginger to marinade for 30 minutes.

3. Skewer pieces of fruit and cook over a barbecue for five minutes turning to cook evenly.

Appendix:
THE FAT AND CALORIE
CONTENTS OF FOOD

All these figures were taken from McCance and Widdowson's *The Composition of Foods* by A. A. Paul and D. A. T. Southgate. Figures show the weight of fat (g) and the number of kilocalories in 100g (4 oz) of the food.

food	fat (g)	calories
Dairy Produce		
Full-fat milk	3.8	65
Skimmed milk	0.1	33
Single cream	21.2	212
Double cream	48.2	447
Whipping cream	35.0	332
Camembert cheese	23.2	300
Cheddar cheese	33.5	406
Danish Blue cheese	29.2	355
Edam	22.9	304
Stilton	40.0	462
Cottage cheese	4.0	96
Cream cheese	47.4	439
Yogurt	1.0	52
Eggs (approx. 2 size 4)	10.9	147
Egg yolk	30.5	339
Egg white	Tr	36

food	fat (g)	calories
Meat		
Bacon		
Grilled gammon rasher, with fat	12.2	228
Grilled streaky rasher, with fat	36.0	422
Beef		
Grilled rump steak, lean and fat	12.1	218
lean only	6.0	168
Stewed mince	16.2	221
Roast sirloin, lean and fat	21.2	284
lean only	9.1	192
Stewed steak, lean and fat	11.0	223
Lamb		
Breast, roast lean and fat	37.1	410
lean only	16.6	252
Cutlets, grilled lean and fat (weighed with bone)	20.4	244
lean only	5.4	97
Leg, roast lean and fat	17.9	266
lean only	8.1	191
Shoulder, roast lean and fat	26.3	316
lean only	11.2	196
Pork		
Belly rashers, grilled lean and fat	34.8	398
Loin chops, grilled lean and fat		
(weighed with bone)	18.8	258
lean only	6.3	133
Leg, roast lean and fat	19.8	286
Veal		
Fillet, roast	11.5	230
Poultry and Game		
Chicken		
Boiled, meat only	7.3	183
Roast, meat only	5.4	148
meat and skin	14.0	216
Leg quarter (weighed with bone)	3.4	92
Duck		
Roast, meat only	9.7	189
meat, fat and skin	29.0	339
Pheasant, roast	9.3	213
Pigeon, roast	13.2	230

food	fat (g)	calories
Turkey		
Roast, meat only	2.7	140
Roast, meat and skin	6.5	171
Rabbit, stewed	7.7	179
Offal		
Lamb kidney, raw	2.7	90
Pig kidney, raw	2.7	90
Ox kidney, raw	2.6	86
Chicken liver, raw	6.3	135
Lamb liver, raw	10.3	179
Pig liver, raw	6.8	154
Meat Products		
Corned beef	12.1	217
Ham	5.1	120
Luncheon meat	26.9	313
Ham and pork, chopped	23.6	270
Liver sausage	26.9	310
Frankfurters	25.0	274
Salami	45.2	491
Beef sausages, fried	18.0	269
grilled	17.3	265
Pork sausages, fried	24.5	317
grilled	24.6	318
Beefburgers, fried	17.3	264
Cornish pasty	20.4	332
Pork pie	27.0	376
Sausage roll	36.2	479
Steak and kidney pie	21.2	323
Fish		
Cod		
Fried in batter	10.3	199
Grilled	1.3	95
Poached	1.1	94
Haddock		
Fried	8.3	174
Steamed	0.8	98
Smoked, steamed	0.9	101

food	fat (g)	calories
Halibut, steamed	4.0	131
Lemon sole		
Fried	13.0	216
Steamed	0.9	91
Plaice		
Fried in batter	18.0	279
Steamed	1.9	93
Herring		
Fried (weighed with bones)	13.3	206
Grilled (weighed with bones)	8.8	135
Kipper, baked (weighed with bones)	6.2	111
Mackerel, fried (weighed with bones)	8.3	138
Salmon, steamed (weighed with bones and skin	10.5	160
Sardines, canned in oil, fish only	13.6	217
Trout, brown, steamed (weighed with bones)	3.0	89
Tuna, canned in oil	22.0	289
Crab, boiled	5.2	127
Prawns, boiled	1.8	107
Scampi, fried	17.6	316
Shrimps, boiled	2.4	117
Scallops, steamed	1.4	105

Cereals

Barley	1.7	360
Wholemeal flour	2.0	318
Oatmeal	8.7	401
Rice	1.0	361
Wholemeal bread	2.7	216
All Bran	5.7	273
Muesli	7.5	368
Shredded Wheat	3.0	324
Weetabix	3.4	340
Rye crispbread	2.1	321

Cakes, Pastries and Biscuits

Digestives	20.5	471
Chocolate digestives	24.1	493
Fruit cake	12.9	354
Doughnuts	15.8	349
Scones	14.6	371

food	fat (g)	calories
Fruit pie	15.5	369

Pulses
Butter beans		
raw	1.1	273
boiled	0.3	95
Haricot beans, raw	1.6	271
Baked beans, canned	0.5	64
Red kidney, raw	1.7	272
Lentils		
raw	1.0	304
boiled	0.5	99
Peas, split		
dried	1.3	286
boiled	0.4	103
Chick peas		
raw	5.7	320
boiled	3.3	144

Nuts
Almonds	53.5	565
Brazil nuts	61.5	619
Chestnuts	2.7	170
Hazelnuts	36.0	380
Coconut, desiccated	62.0	604
Peanuts		
fresh	36.0	351
roasted and salted	49.0	570
Walnuts	51.5	525

Vegetables: raw unless otherwise stated (Tr = Trace)
Asparagus	Tr	18
Aubergine	Tr	14
French beans	Tr	7
Runner beans	0.2	26
Broad beans	0.6	48
Beetroot	Tr	28
Broccoli tops	Tr	23
Brussels sprouts	Tr	26
Spring cabbage (boiled)	Tr	7

food	fat (g)	calories
Carrots	Tr	23
Cauliflower	Tr	13
Celery	Tr	8
Cucumber	Tr	10
Leeks	Tr	31
Lettuce	0.4	12
Marrow	Tr	16
Mushrooms	0.6	13
Onions	Tr	23
Parsnips	Tr	49
Peas	0.4	67
Potatoes	0.4	87
mashed	5.0	119
roast	4.8	157
chipped	10.9	253
crisps	35.9	533
Spinach (boiled)	0.5	30
Swede	Tr	21
Sweetcorn on the cob	2.4	127
Sweetcorn kernels, canned	0.5	76
Tomatoes	Tr	14
Watercress	Tr	14

Fruits

Apples	Tr	46
Apricots	Tr	28
dried	Tr	182
Avocado pears	22.2	223
Bananas	0.3	79
Blackberries	Tr	29
Cherries	Tr	47
Blackcurrants	Tr	28
Currants, dried	Tr	243
Dates, dried	Tr	248
Figs, green	Tr	41
Gooseberries	Tr	17
Grapes, black	Tr	61
Grapefruit	Tr	22
Melon	Tr	24
Olives	11.0	103

food	fat (g)	calories
Oranges	Tr	35
Peaches	Tr	37
Pears	Tr	41
Pineapple, fresh	Tr	46
Plums	Tr	38
Prunes	Tr	161
Raisins	Tr	246
Raspberries	Tr	25
Rhubarb	Tr	6
Strawberries	Tr	26
Sultanas	Tr	250

Miscellaneous

	fat (g)	calories
Chocolate, milk	30.3	529
Mayonnaise	78.9	718
Sweet pickle	0.3	134
Salad cream	27.4	311
Ice-cream	6.6	167

INDEX